1116
This edition published in 1991 by Tiger Books International PLC, London
© Coombe Books
Printed and bound in Singapore
All rights reserved
ISBN 1 85501 128 X

THE COMPLETE BOOK OF
MAKE UP &
HAIRCARE

PAT SPIRES AND SARAH COLLINS

**TIGER BOOKS INTERNATIONAL
LONDON**

Contents

Introduction

It is not an overstatement to say that every woman has her own kind of beauty. It is, however, very true to say that there are many who are unsure about how to make the best of that natural beauty and don't know about the enormous psychological boost that making the most of yourself gives you.

With some, it's a natural shyness – a feeling that wearing make-up would make them seem different from their normal selves. For others, it's more a question of not really knowing how to use cosmetics in the right way that leads them to ignore the make-up counters in the stores. Yet the art of making up is not to change but to create illusions; to enhance, to disguise and it is very simple and easy to learn.

In the pages of this book there are make-ups for everyone. We have set out to show you just some of the thousands of different ways that make-up can be made to work for you. Some of the ideas may shock, some may even seem a little dull, but they are there to show you graphically some of the magic to encourage you to be more adventurous, to get you out of a rut or just to give you some new ideas to try out.

3

Above *Sally has a classically pretty face – good shape, high cheekbones, almond shaped eyes that are not too big and certainly not too small, a straight unprominent nose and full lips. We purposely left her hair slicked back and away from her face so that the real dramatic effects created by make-up are shown even more graphically.*

1: *Sleek and elegant with muted shades.*

2: *Clashing colours used to stunning effect.*

3: *Disco glitter and colour.*

2

Tough, strong and theatrical.

Cats eyes sensation.

Clashing oranges and blues can go
together.

Fresh and pretty with fake freckles.

over girl glamour.

Outdoor fresh and natural.

egant sixties shape and shade.

Sculptured and sensational.

Chapter 1

The Bare Canvas

Just as a beautiful painting starts life on a clean fresh canvas, so too a good make-up starts from a clear, clean complexion. Of course it's a rare person that has a completely trouble-free skin but problems can be minimised by following the time-worn ritual of cleanse, tone and moisturise night and morning and always before applying make-up.

Learn to recognise your skin type, it's either dry, greasy or a combination of the two with a greasy panel down the centre of the face. Select skincare products to suit and religiously use them. Get plenty of fresh air; eat as many fresh fruits and green vegetables as you can and avoid fried foods, to aid a healthy clear complexion.

Facial Movement

Treat the skin on your face gently, don't ever tug or pull it, it's very delicate and you'll only encourage wrinkles or broken veins. Use only fingertips to massage and follow these movements whether applying makeup, cleansing, toning or moisturising.

1: *Upward, sweeping movements from the collar bone up the neck.*

2: *Upward and outward from the chin to the temples.*

needs medical treatment. (Skin with clinical acne tends to look very bumpy, red, and often has a certain amount of scaling too – very different from a normal teenage spotty skin.) Sadly, doctors have not yet found the complete answer to acne and the treatments are many and various. On a happier note, in most cases, acne does decrease with age and often goes completely by mid-teens.

Wrinkles Well, they come to us all in time, but a good skincare routine can help a great deal to keep them at bay. Wrinkles start to happen as your skin loses its natural elasticity anytime from the age of thirty onwards. Keep them under control by moisturising and watching for some of the danger signs: dryness; frowning; pulling the skin; too much sun.

3: *Stroking, gentle movements down the centre of the nose.*

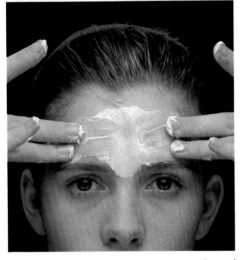

4: *From centre of forehead upwards and out along the forehead.*

Spotting Trouble

Spots It's a pretty rare person who doesn't get the odd spot and they are very annoying, but not always impossible to deal with. Keep your skin as clean as possible and apply the type of spot cream or lotion that contains benzoyl peroxide to dry it out quickly. Never squeeze a spot because the bacteria that cause the spot can spread and encourage another eruption elsewhere on the face. Providing you have treated the spot with cream, then you can safely cover it with make-up to disguise.

Clinical Acne This can be a very real problem for some, especially young teenagers. This should not be confused with normal teenage spots as it usually

5: *Gentle circular movements around the eyes.*

Broken Veins Fair complexions of soft, fine skin are particularly prone to suffering from broken veins – tiny little red lines that occur on the side of the nose and cheeks. They are caused by

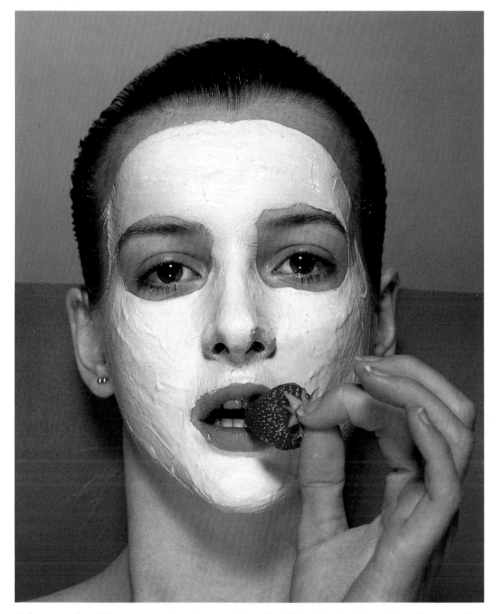

A face mask will leave your skin clear and refreshed: refining pores and removing wrinkles.

---

various outside influences namely a) no protection from excessive sun and wind. b) too much alcohol. c) rough treatment like squeezing, pulling and tugging of the skin. As it's practically impossible to rid yourself of them once they've appeared prevention is a much better idea. Therefore, avoid their occurrence by protecting your face with moisturiser and foundation if you live a healthy outdoor life. Avoid drinking to excess and even eating too much spicey food and treat your face gently.

Blackheads Blackheads and greasy skin tend to go hand in hand. They are caused by the pores becoming blocked with the skin's natural lubricant, sebum. The characteristic black spot that gives them their name is the sebum oxidising in the air, not dirt as is commonly thought. To prevent their occurrence, every time you cleanse simply massage more carefully around the greasy panels and take care to clear the pores with skin tonic when you've finished.

Use this method to prevent and dislodge blackheads that have already formed. A once a week face mask also helps a great deal. But, please, never squeeze a blackhead.

Whiteheads These tend to form around the eyes. They look exactly like blackheads, but, because they are under the skin, the black spot never forms. They are caused by sebum too, but it has become blocked under the skin. One of the reasons that they form is cleansing with the wrong product and heavy oil used to remove make-up is often blamed for them. You cannot remove them yourself and the best method is to go to a beauty salon for an electrolysis treatment.

Avoid the occurrence of whiteheads by using only specialised eye make-up remover, cleansing cream or lotion.

Enlarged Pores This problem is often known as 'orange peel skin' because that's exactly what it looks like – the outer skin of an orange. This happens most commonly on greasy skin and really there is very little that can be done about it except regular toning and having a weekly face mask to help refine the pores.

Superfluous Hair Dark haired people often suffer this problem. We all have hair covering our faces but sometimes it just happens to show more. If your particular problem is fine, dark hair on the upper lip then regular treatment with a facial bleach is a good idea. Thicker, dark hair on cheeks and upper lips can be more of a problem though and there are three possible courses of action 1) Bleaching. 2) Depilation, use a mild facial depilatory once every three weeks or so. 3) Permanent removal with a course of electrolysis. If you choose the first two methods, patch test a small area of skin on the inside of your arm first to make sure that you don't have an allergic reaction. If you select the final course of action, make sure that you go to a beauty therapist who is a registered electrolysis practitioner and ask how long the treatment is liable to take as this can be pretty costly.

Allergies It's not at all uncommon for us all at some time or another to suffer an allergic reaction to the products that we use and this can manifest itself in many different ways. Tiny red spots that itch, a burning rash and swelling are all sure signs of an allergy. Often it's nothing to do with the make-up you're using but more likely to be caused by something you ate, a form of hay fever, nerves or even a new perfume you're wearing. But if you do get an allergy, it's best to watch your cleansing and make-up routine by switching to hypo-allergenic and perfume free products until it has abated.

Home Beauty Treatments

Even the most trouble free of complexions needs an occasional lift to help revitalise and rejuvenate. And, one of the quickest and most effective ways of doing this is to treat yourself to a face mask. This will help refine pores, iron out tiny wrinkles and leave your skin clear and refreshed.

If you go to a beauty salon for a professional facial a major part of the treatment will involve rest and relaxation. Therefore, before embarking on an at-home facial it's a must to make sure that, for at least fifteen minutes, you are free from interruption. Lock the door and take the phone off the hook. Run a warm bath, cleanse your face thoroughly and while you're freshly bathed and wrapped in a warm towel put on your chosen mask. Set your alarm to ring in ten

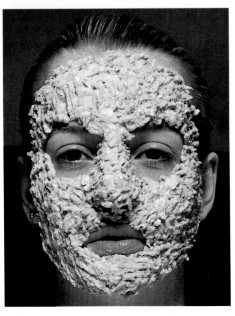

minutes and lie back and relax with cotton wool pads wrung out in cold water, or cucumber slices, over your eyes. When your time is up, thoroughly rinse off all traces of the mask and splash your face with cool water to tone.

There is an enormous variety of branded face masks to choose from, suited to all skin types but your larder too contains the makings for your own home-made kind that can work just as efficiently. Cucumber is wonderful for skin. Simply cover your face with slices and let the oil soak in. Sliced or pulped strawberries are beautiful too if a little costly. But for a highly effective quick lift, there's nothing better than the skin of a fresh pineapple – the inside juicy part of course. Pineapple, apart from being

really best to stick to unperfumed facial soap and once a week gently slough away dead skin by using a man's clean shaving brush or special cosmetic brush. Remember always though that soap must be thoroughly rinsed away as a residue on the skin can cause excessive dryness and itching.

Sparkling Eyes

Because they are the visible, living part of you, care of your eyes is very important indeed. Of course it goes without saying that sleep is one of the best beauty treatments not only for your eyes but your whole body too – eight hours a

Sparkling healthy eyes are perhaps the greatest aid to beauty, so care for them well.

---

delicious to eat is packed full of living enzymes that are said to work miracles on tired skin.

If you've been making fresh mayonnaise, don't throw away the egg white. Instead, whisk it up and pat it gently onto the face, leave for ten minutes and rinse off with cold water – a lovely pick-me-up.

It's a pretty sobering fact that the only living part of the human body that is visible is the eyes. The rest is in fact dead, as the living skin is under a fine layer of

dead cells that are constantly being lost and replaced from below. Normal cleansing and washing helps to peel the old dead skin away but sometimes a little encouragement is needed to avoid clogging pores and the characteristic sallowness of tired skin. This is known as exfoliation. Face masks do this job very well but oily skins can also benefit from a once a week wash with a granular cleanser. This type of cleanser is usually called a 'facial scrub' and contains tiny granules. In fact, fine ground oatmeal mixed to a paste with water and gently massaged in circular movements is also an extremely efficient exfoliator.

If you're a soap and water addict it's

night is the ideal but not always possible. But continual late nights will soon start to show, with tiny strain lines and perhaps puffiness all around your eyes.

The area around your eyes is the most delicate on the body so the 'no tugging or pulling' rule is even more important here. A useful tip is only to use your little finger to apply make-up or creams to avoid exerting too much pressure on this area. Keep face masks, exfoliating aids and heavy creams away from your eyes too. If you are starting to get fine lines and wrinkles, gently massage in a special eye cream nightly, try to relax as much as possible and have your eyes tested; you may need glasses.

Chapter 2
The Basics

The old saying 'a workman is only as good as his tools' is very true of the difference between being professional about your make-up or just plain amateur. Don't be frightened by our picture of the contents of a professional make-up kit; I just wanted to show you the infinite variety of kinds of cosmetics and aids that are available. But this should at the same time give you some idea of

Just a small portion of a professional make-up kit to show the infinite variety of cosmetics that are on the market including products from: Revlon, Maybelline, Max Factor, Boots, Cover Girl Lancôme, Helena Rubenstein and Miners.

the variety of cosmetics and tools needed to create the myriad different looks and styles that you can see in the pages of this book.

Although most cosmetics manufacturers supply brushes and applicators with their products, there is really no substitute for some of the more professional ones that make making-up a much simpler process. Also, the many

different formulations of products suit different techniques and lifestyles. Learn these techniques and learn how to apply the products successfully and making-up is going to be so much easier to do.

Starting Right

Here's a list of the basic items that you will need before starting work:—

1. **Tissues** – For cleansing and correcting mistakes, nothing else will do.

2. **Cotton Buds** – Invaluable for mopping-up eye and lip make-up mistakes.

3. **Cotton Wool** – For using damp to remove cleanser from the skin and to apply toner before moisturising.

4. **Brushes and applicators** – You need at least five. Choose a big fat one for blushing and shaping; two are needed for eyes, one shaped and one soft and fat for all over shading; a sponge tip applicator is very useful for applying pressed powder and cream shadows too; a lip brush is a must especially for outlining and smoother and longer lasting application.

5. **Cosmetic Sponge**– For even application of foundation, there is no substitute.

Make sure that everything that touches your face is clean and never use the first three items more than once, they're disposable so dispose of them the minute they've been used. Wash your brushes and applicators at least once a week in mild soapy water, rinse very well, gently pull them back into shape and let them dry overnight.

Your Cosmetic Kit

Are you one of those ladies who are putty in the hands of a good cosmetic sales lady? If you are then you probably have a drawer-full of products that you have either no idea how to use or no wish to use in the first place. I'm a great believer in having a whole wardrobe of

make-up on hand to cover every eventuality. But, for normal everyday wear there are really only a few items that you really do need to see you through. Open up your drawer and select items from this list because this is really all you need.

1. **Foundation** – Cake and cream foundations are best suited to dry or problem (spotty) skins; the mat cream types often called 'complete make-up suit combination and oily skin types. If your skin is normal, the cream type suits well.

2. **Cover Stick** – To hide dark shadows, spots and mild blemishes, cover sticks

are invaluable. Although they are formulated to cover spots they work wonders on disguising all manner of problems.

3. **Translucent Powder** – A must for setting your foundation, it's lighter and more controllable than pressed powder.

4. **Blusher** – Choose the type that suits your chosen foundation – creams are best used on top of cream and cake foundations and powders work well on 'complete' foundations.

5. **Shadows** – Whatever shape your eyes you're going to need at least three different shades to create the right kind of effect.

6. **Kohl Pencil** – Very useful for defining shape and even using in place of eye shadow for a quick make-up.

7. **Mascara** – Probably the most important cosmetic of all to enhance the natural beauty of your eyes.

8. **Eyebrow Pencil & Tweezers** – Use your tweezers to pluck stray hairs and neaten the shape, and a pencil to emphasise.

9. **Lipstick** – You'll need at least three different shades to suit every mood, occasion and outfit.

The Technique

The great art in making-up is to do it so well that it will last all day without constant re-touching. With all the various forms that cosmetics take and the many different formulations it is often a case of trial and error to choose a brand that really suits you. It is also a case of learning how to apply the different formulations in the correct way to make them last.

The Base

If you are one of those lucky few who are blessed with a perfect skin with even colouring then you will not need to use a foundation – just moisturise and carry on to the next stage of making up. If, on the other hand, you are like the majority of the population, your skin tones will need evening-up to make the perfect base. Choose your shade very carefully. Make use of the manufacturers' testers and apply a little to the back of your hand and check it in daylight. Ideally, the colour should exactly match your skin tones; failing that, choose a shade slightly darker but never lighter. Very dark skinned people often have trouble finding a foundation that's the right shade, in which case you should mix your own by blending two matching foundations together to achieve the right tones. The best way of doing this is to buy the same type and brand of products and mix them in an empty container (it's just like mixing paint).

Always apply foundation sparingly to avoid looking caked. Dot all over the face and neck and blend with a slightly dampened cosmetic sponge, remembering to use upward movements. When it's completely even, very gently finish off using downward movements so that the hairs on your face lie flat.

Covering Up Use your cover stick to

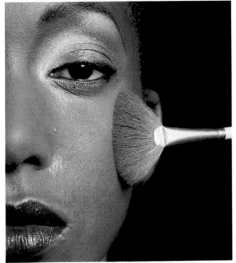

camouflage blemishes, and shadows under your eyes. Choose a shade lighter than your foundation and apply to the area to be hidden with your fingertip and blend with a clean brush.

Powdering Up To help set your foundation and provide a grease-free base for make-up, powder is a must and translucent powder is the easiest and most effective form to buy. Apply using a clean cotton wool ball and press gently onto the skin; when your face is covered, dust off the excess with the clean side of the cotton wool using downward movements to keep the hairs lying flat.

Blushing There are essentially three forms of blusher: gel, cream and powder.

If you prefer to use either gel or cream this should be applied before powdering. Simply dot the area to be shaded and blend carefully with fingertips. For powder blusher use a nice fat brush for even blending after powdering.

Make your blusher work for you to enhance your face shape – it's not there to add colour – it's there to create an illusion. The first rule to remember is that of light and shade. Use lighter shades (highlighters) to enhance your best features like cheekbones and darker shades to give the impression of depth and to hide.

The shades of blusher that you should choose really depend on your natural colouring. If for instance you have very olive skin, bright pinks just won't suit at all and shades of brown would look pretty wrong on a peaches and cream complexion. Ideally, too, the colour should never clash with your chosen outfit.

I have mentioned highlighters in this section because they are useful for helping to enhance your good natural features. Often, rather than buying a separate highlighter, powder eye shadow works just as well providing you choose pale peach, ivory or gold (this looks wonderful with a tan).

Remember that your face is rounded with no angular lines so always blend blusher and highlighter well and never colour in straight lines, to keep the look as natural as possible.

Eye Shadow There are pressed powders, creams, loose powders, cream and powder mixed, and pencils for you to choose from and there is a different technique for applying each one.

The most popular form of eye shadow is pressed powder; there's a huge colour variety to choose from and they really are the easiest to apply and have good lasting ability. Use either a brush or sponge tip applicator for best results.

Cream shadows are very suited to those with dry skin and should be applied with a sponge applicator.

You literally draw the outline you need and then soften and blend using a stubby eyeshadow brush. A light dusting of translucent powder on top will help to maintain lasting ability.

Ideally, your pencils should have quite a good point and, because they are so soft, it's easy to break them when sharpening. To overcome this simply put your pencil in the refrigerator for about twenty minutes before sharpening and allow it to warm up again before applying to lids. This tip is also useful for sharpening kohl pencils.

When choosing colours you will need three basic shades, all complementing each other – a pale frosted shade for highlighting, a deep shade for shaping

Loose powder shadows usually offer the brightest colours but can be tricky to apply. If using straight from the pot, a sponge applicator helps even application but, mixed with a little water on the back of the hand and applied with a brush, I find that they last longer.

Powder and cream mixes come with their own applicator. This form of eye shadow is probably the most durable and is very often waterproof too. They are very fast drying so blend with your fingertip straight after application.

Pencils Soft, eye pencils can produce some very interesting effects. Because they are soft and slightly greasy, they are best suited to dry and combination skins.

and avoid clogging on upper lashes – look upward for lower lashes. Brush on the lashes finely with separate coats for a soft, natural look.

Kohl Pencil The softest and easiest kind of eyeliner to use, kohl (sometimes known as kajal) pencils are perfect for defining eye shape and as a quick substitute for eye shadow. Using light movements, you draw a line and then blend with a brush to give a natural, soft shape.

Brow Shaping Your eyes need a frame to balance and your brows are that natural frame. Take care when plucking to let them keep their natural shape. Use a pencil to measure for perfect shape brows:– 1. Hold pencil vertical on line with the inner corner of your eye – your brow should stop at this line. 2. Hold

and a medium shade to add dimension. The colour range that you choose is very important too. For a beginners kit, you can't go far wrong with shades of beige, brown and copper – these suit practically all eye and fashion colours as they are fairly neutral. Don't believe the old adage that blues suit blue eyes and browns hazel and brown eyes: it's just not true.

Mascara All eyelashes need accentuating with mascara even if they are dark and thick. Choose a shade close to your own lash colour (blondes should never wear black) and apply carefully. Hold your mirror so that you look down into it and zigzag the brush to separate pencil by your nostril diagonally across to the outer corner of your eye – the brow line should end here.

Brows always look best natural rather than over plucked. Using a baby's toothbrush or brow-brush, shape and tweeze only stray hairs that spoil the natural outline – gently hold the skin taut between fore and middle fingers and pluck outwards with the natural hair growth.

Always use a sharp brow pencil and draw small feathery strokes that look just like real hair.

Lipstick Once upon a time, this was woman's 'only' cosmetic. Now lipstick is there to complete the whole facial picture with soft, muted colours and gloss to make you look natural, and clear, bright colours to turn you into an instant glamour picture.

It's wise to choose three shades to complement your mood and outfit and, here again, beware of choosing clashing colours. For instance, orange lips and purple or blue eyes just don't work – soft, bluey pinks suit much better. Similarly, true pink lips just don't match soft brown eye shades.

Let your lipstick match your mood.

Chapter 3
So who's got Problems?

There's practically no woman on this earth who is the perfect beauty; life just isn't like that. The stunning models who stare out at you from the pages of the magazines, the glorious stars who waft across the movie screens and even your best friend who always manages to look that bit more beautiful than you, all probably have their problems – they're just well disguised, that's all!

In the pages of this book you'll see, in some of the step-by-step pictures, spots being hidden, dark shadows being painted out and all manner of tricks that can be used to camouflage. Yet in the final picture, you'll notice that there's not a trace of a flaw. This isn't a result of special lighting techniques, it's just clever make-up. No matter what your particular problem may be, there are ways of hiding it without changing yourself drastically in any way. This is important to remember because, no matter what your make-up does for you, it should always mirror you and your personality and never try to turn you into something you are not.

Before starting work you will need to be totally honest with yourself. Place your mirror in a good natural light – it should always be there to ensure a perfect make-up – pull your hair away from your un-made-up face and take a good look. Yours' may be beautiful eyes or a perfect shape nose. Now look for the flaws like scars, blemishes, pointed nose, small eyes. All that you need to do now is learn to enhance your good points and disguise your bad – simple when you know how.

Spots and Blemishes In theory spots should be allowed to dry out naturally but nowadays certain preparations will work on this with or without foundation on top. As has been mentioned before, choose a cream or lotion containing Benzoyl Peroxide – your chemist will point you in the right direction – apply a little directly onto the spot, smooth in and allow to dry completely and then apply foundation all over. Minor spots will be hidden by just this but those awful, once-a month kind still tend to show through. Hide them by simply dabbing on the area with a cover stick in a shade paler than your foundation. Now, using a clean brush, blend the colour into the surrounding area.

Acne Most acne sufferers use special medicated products prescribed by a doctor to help with the problem. It's therefore a good idea to check with him whether make-up will affect the treatment in any way. If you get the go-ahead to wear make-up then you'll find a great ally in green cover cream. This is just like it sounds: it's the colour green and is perfect for blotting out the red colour that is so often associated with acne. Apply over the effected area with a clean sponge before covering with a light foundation. Don't be tempted to use a cake or stick foundation as this will tend to clog on the uneven parts of the skin and show up the imperfections all the more. Any red marks that can still be seen can then be covered by using the same method described in the Spots and Blemishes section.

High Colouring and Broken Veins It's so easy to disguise high colouring that it almost doesn't merit a mention here. But fine, pale skins do tend to have the problem of getting a little rosy especially when hot, and many do find it very embarrassing. Fine skin is also prone to broken veins especially on the cheek area. Therefore, anyone who has this type of complexion should pay a great deal of attention to protection with moisturiser and foundation, as exposure to harsh weather is often the principal cause of broken veins. Both problems, however, are quickly and simply hidden with the useful green cover cream applied under your normal make-up.

Wrinkles Laughter lines, frown lines, crow's feet, call them what you will, they come to us all in the end but they can be kept at bay by following a good skin care regime. It's now also generally felt that too much sun can be ageing so it's wise to take care when tanning to give your face extra protection too.

To diminish lines that are already there, you simply use a cover stick a shade lighter than your normal foundation colour. With a fine brush you paint along the wrinkle line then, using feathery strokes blend into the surrounding area.

Dark Shadows & Baggy Eyes Both these problems are often a sure sign of insufficient sleep. However, there are quite a few women who always suffer from one or the other no matter how many hours sleep they get. Here again, a light coloured cover stick or cake foundation, painted over the area and blended, will fade away dark shadows. Bags under the eyes can be diminished by painting or blending a slightly deeper shade of foundation over the area. A shading or dark brown kohl pencil under the lid also adds to the disguise.

Face Shaping It is said that the perfect face is heart shaped with forehead and cheekbones the same width, tapering to a well proportioned chin. In addition to this there are three other basic shapes – oval, round and square and we all fall into one of these categories. Each individual shape needs shading and highlighting in a different way to improve the proportions.

The rule of light to enhance and shade to diminish is used to best effect in basic face shaping. Therefore use a deep toned blusher to disguise a prominent chin or nose as well as to improve the

face shape. If you're blessed with good basic bone structure, use a highlighter to bring it out even more. Use a face shaping brush to apply highlighter – it's like a blusher brush but with slightly shorter, more stubby bristles. If you are using a cream highlighter, apply and blend with fingertips. Pay very special attention to avoid harsh unblended lines and follow the natural curving contours of your face.

1: Heart Shape *This is a very simple face to shape. Look in your mirror and grin. Your face will make a natural indentation just below your cheek bone and this where you should apply your blusher. Gently find your cheekbones with fingertips and apply your highlighter along this line, brushing or smoothing with your fingertips to blend naturally with your blusher.*

2: Oval Shape *You will need to create a false shape by shading over the cheek area and taking your blusher right up to your temples to give a slimmer effect. Here too, blend highlighter upwards and outwards along the line of your cheek bone.*

3: Round Shape *If your face is very rounded you need to give it a slimmed*

down effect. For the best effect you need two shades of blusher in the same colour tones. Use the lighter of the two shades first over the cheek area right down to your jaw line but fading away before reaching the temples. Blend the deeper shade around the edge of your face and into the centre of the cheek area. Highlight your cheek bone only until you are on line with the outer corners of your eyes. You can diminish a double chin by hiding with the lighter of your two blushers too.

4: Square Shape *Soften the angular line of your face by applying blusher in the centre of the cheek area and blending highlighter on the edge of your face. A little blusher on each side of the forehead will also give more shape and dimension.*

Girls With Glasses

Making-up for wearing glasses can be a little tricky, especially if you're very short sighted. Difficult it may be but impossible it certainly is not. Here, more than ever you really do need a good light and you need a large, magnifying mirror too. Keep your glasses to hand and, after finishing each stage,

1

pop them on and check out how you are doing in a normal mirror. Because they are going to be slightly hidden behind glass, you will need to emphasise your eyes even more to show them to best effect. Choose eye shades that complement the colour of your frames and follow the frame shape when shading – our photos here show you the importance of this.

Contact Lenses

Many people who wear contact lenses tend to have some difficulty in using eye make-up. Often eyes become sensitive and great care must be taken not to let any foreign bodies drop into the eyes.

It's a good idea to cut down the risk of sensitivity by selecting eye make-up that is hypo-allergenic and thus less likely to

2

1: *Pretty girl, pretty frames but, wearing the minimum of eye make-up does look rather plain and dull.*

2: *Notice the difference. Now, with blending tones of burgundy, pink and brown, her eyes look really stunning; really singing out from behind the glasses.*

cause irritation. If you have soft lenses, put them in before making-up but, if you wear hard lenses, insert them after you've

finished. Take care when removing your make-up too, tissues or dampened cotton wool are essential for this in order to avoid stray fibres getting in the eye.

It's best to stick to using cream, pressed powder or automatic eye shadow for shading but if you prefer to use loose powder mix it with water before brushing onto lids. Fibreless mascara and the softest of pencils are a must too and, anyone wearing contact lenses should avoid pencilling on the insides of lids.

Lip Service

No beautiful face is complete without lipstick and, as with all make-up techniques, there are rights and wrongs about the colours you choose as well as the application. As far as colour is concerned, it should never clash with your chosen outfit and should blend well with your chosen eye shadow shades. For the best and most long-lasting application, apply with a brush, blot with a tissue and re-apply. A light dusting with translucent powder before putting it on will also help to keep lips colourful longer.

There are a lucky few who are blessed with perfect lip proportions – fairly generous size, slightly turned up at the corners, a rounded cupid's bow and uniform size of top and bottom lips. If, on the other hand, your lip shape is not quite perfect, don't worry, there are very simple ways to fake the right shape. For lips that are too wide, you simply make a false

shape within the natural line of your lips. Cover the edges of your mouth with foundation, then using a lip brush, draw an outline that ends before it reaches the corners. Fill in the fake outline with the same colour. Slimline lips need a little more disguise. Many feel that application of colour outside the natural lip line is a good idea, but in practice this can result in smudging. Instead, outline

the natural shape with a pale shade and fill in with a slightly darker but toning lipstick colour. Avoid bright shades as these will only help to emphasise the thin shape. Although very attractive to some, many feel that full generous lips are not their cup of tea. Slim down by simply outlining with a deep shade of lip pencil just inside the natural line and fill in with your chosen lipstick, avoiding very pale or very bright colours. If your problem is badly matched lips, i.e. full bottom lip, thin top lip, you'll need two lipsticks in toning light and dark shades. Emphasise the smaller lip by applying pale foundation around its natural outline and then, using the paler shade

With confidence you can create many different moods.

paint the lip following the natural outline. Colour the fuller lip inside the natural line with the deeper shade. To finish the illusion blend a little of the paler shade on the centre where the two lips meet so that the difference between the shades you've used won't be noticeable.

Eyes Right

Learning the art of eye disguise is quite simple but probably the most important technique that you ever have to learn. Your eyes, apart from being the only visible 'living' part of your body, are your most important asset. Even if you have the most beautiful figure, or the longest legs, it's a known fact that anyone meeting you will look you in the eyes first.

It matters not whether your eyes are big, small, deep set or protruding, eye make-up will help to compensate for all problems. The same principles that have applied for face and lip shaping work well on eyes too – light colours bring out and deep shades give shape and dimension.

1: *Here we see Susie. She has small, slightly uptilting eyes with a good basic shape and rich colour – without makeup they are just a nice pair of slightly unremarkable eyes.*

2: *This attempt at making up has failed miserably. In trying to emphasise their shape, she has drawn harsh black lines with a kohl pencil and dabbed on a nondescript pale blue shadow. The effect is to make her eyes look smaller and too strongly slanted.*

3: *Clever shading creates a dramatic and prominent eye shape. Pale pink shadow applied at inner corners gives extra width and this is smoothed just under the brow line to add shape. All the rest of the*

1 **2**

3

4

5

6

shading is achieved with a black kohl pencil. A line is drawn all around each eye and taken straight out at each corner instead of upwards to hide the slant. Using a good eyeshadow brush, the line is feathered to create the shading effect. To give extra dimension, white eye crayon has been drawn along the inner rim of lower lids before mascara was applied –

this gives an instant wide effect.

4: Here we see a perfect example of prominent, wide-set eyes; eyes that are just crying out to be made up and enhanced.

5: Light shadow at inner corners of eyes spaces them too far apart and the winged eyeliner just does nothing to shape,

succeeding in making the look very dated.

6: See how the use of a deep sable shadow gives drama and creates a wonderfully sultry effect. A rich copper shadow brushed right up to the nose immediately brings those wide-set eyes closer together and gives better proportion.

Chapter 4
Young Looks

The teens and early twenties are really the most exciting time for making up, especially now, when fashion-wise literally anything goes. And, whatever you do, providing you do it with style, you can get away with it, Some of the more way-out looks can, it must be said, look downright ugly but many can look very spectacular and history always shows that this is the age of experimentation.

1: *Debbie came into our photographic studio, a fresh faced girl just starting life as a model and ready to be transformed. We selected her because she has all the potential of a pretty girl who could be quite easily turned into a stunner.*

2: *Her softly permed hair is twisted in small sections and pinned to give more curl and bounce.*

3: *Debbie has a problem – too many late nights have given her black bags under her eyes. A pale cover stick is painted over the area and blended.*

4: There's no avoiding the odd spot – this one is quickly hidden with cover stick too.

5: A light, lotion foundation is gently patted with a cosmetic sponge all over the face to even colouring.

6: Translucent powder is applied liberally all over with cotton wool and the excess brushed away with a complexion brush.

7: Soft kohl pencil outlines Debbie's almond shape eyes.

8: The kohl line is softened with a brush.

9: Deep pink pressed powder shadow is applied to the upper lid and blended with a deep purple applied at outer corners and above the crease line.

10: A pale, frosted pink is brushed just under the brow line to emphasise the eye shape.

11: Debbie's eyebrows are quite dark and free of straggly hairs so they are just simply brushed into shape – no pencilling is necessary.

12: Eyes are given the final touch with two coats of brownish-black mascara.

13: A soft pink blusher co-ordinates with Debbie's eye shades. It's brushed just under the cheek bone and out towards the temples.

As in all things it's a good idea to remember the old adage, 'don't run before you can walk'. In other words, learn the basics first and then you'll be much more expert at attempting the unusual. Start by perfecting a natural look that enhances your good points, then try out some more fun ideas when you

3

know yourself and the techniques much better.

Answering the question 'When should I start to use make-up?' is rather like trying to answer 'How long is a piece of string?' because opinion varies. The only way I can give any kind of answer is to say that there's a time and a place for everything. Heavy black eyes and bright pink lips certainly look pretty silly at school but lovely in a disco. Similarly blusher and powder look fairly ridiculous on a day out in the country but perfectly suitable for a job in a bank. Sometimes it's a bitter pill to swallow, but you really should learn to be adaptable and create the right look for the right time.

14

15

14: *A soft lip-liner provides a clear outline for lipstick.*

15: *Vivid pink lipstick put on with a brush will last longer.*

16: *The finished effect shows just how make-up has emphasised Debbie's beautiful assets. Eyes have more shape from the clever use of kohl and the upward sweep of shadow. Her lovely high cheek bones are more visible now with blusher brushed underneath.*

1: Jo, just like many teenagers loves trying out new fashion and make-up ideas and spent many happy hours in our studio with a hairdresser and make-up artist discussing cosmetic possibilities. Here, her face is clean and ready to start work. Too much partying has left her with very bad black shadows under her well shaped green eyes and she had a few spots on her chin too. Both problems were quickly hidden under a painting of cover stick and a light application of cream foundation.

1

2: Looking every inch a girl about to go to her first dance, we gave full emphasis to Jo's eyes for this look. Pale plum shadow is brushed all over top lids following a curving line from outer corners up to the brow. Navy blue kohl pencil outlines the shape and is brushed outwards to blend naturally into the plum shade. A little pale, frosted blue is added at inner corners to define the line. Here you can see clearly how contrasting colours succeed in making her eyes appear even greener than they naturally are. Blusher and lipstick are deliberately neutral in order not to detract attention from the eyes.

2

3: Shades of apricot and gold give Jo a real cover-girl look, yet this make-up is simplicity itself. Using just one colour shadow in a deep apricot shade, the shape of Jo's eyes is brought out by delicately shading with a frosted brown shadow crayon. Note, too, how the shadow is taken right up to the bridge of her nose to reduce the flattened effect. Gold glitter is painted over the whole upper lid area for the extra sparkle. Burnt orange-gold lips echo the complete gilded effect.

Overleaf: A pre-Raphaelite hairdo and stunning colours turn Jo into a budding pop star in a matter of minutes. Deep cerise shadow teamed with frosted aqua and navy liner would normally clash horribly; here they create a truly dramatic effect. Blusher and lips in toning vibrant pink add to a look that is certainly not for the shy or faint-hearted and perfect for the extrovert.

1: *Ling Tai is an extremely pretty young Chinese girl with a very classic face. If you analyse her features you will find that she has a round face shape, a broad, slightly flat nose, characteristically small, almond shape eyes and full lips.*

2: This attempt at making up has made some classic mistakes. Her foundation is far too pale, her brows overdrawn. Sparkling blue shadow follows and emphasises the eye shape and the heavy black line literally closes them up. Her pink blusher certainly shapes her face and matches the cyclamen coloured lipstick but just creates the feeling that Ling is an over-painted doll.

3: Now, see how a pretty girl can be turned into a beautiful one. A toning foundation has softened her look instantly. Just look at those eyes too. Peach frosted shadow has been applied all over lids, and charcoal grey painted at inner corners gives shape to the bridge of her nose. The same charcoal brushed under lower lids and out at the sides gives extra width. Soft amber blusher creates a more sculptured effect and is also used to help shape her nose, by dusting a little down each side. A warm, ginger-tone, glossy lipstick brings out the natural roundness of her lips.

1: This lovely, classic English Rose keeps her look simple for daytime. Natural shades of peach and soft rose for lips and cheeks and a light smudging of dark brown kohl pencil to accentuate her eyes create a perfect, soft and young look.

2: Classic features need little make-up change for a glamour evening look. A light, soft pink highlighter gives extra dimension to the eyes. Lip colour is strengthened and a slick of gloss is added. Clever accessorising with a headband made from twisted ribbon and material scraps give her extra nighttime style.

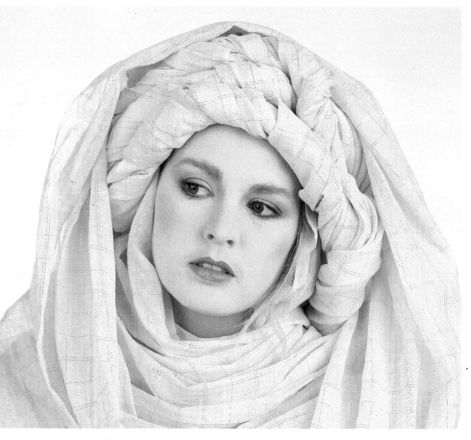

1: *Eye shades of khaki and pewter blend perfectly with this stunning evening dress. Amber blusher and pale toffee coloured lips tone with this beautifully co-ordinated look.*

2: *Identical twins, identically made-up with a look to turn most heads in their direction.*

3: *See how a make-up change can make identical twins look completely different? Here's an example of day and night looks for lookalike people.*

4: *A fantasy of twisted scarves frames a dramatic make-up. Foundation is kept deliberately light coloured to accentuate those stunning eyes.*

1: *Light foundation, brilliant pink blusher and shades of blue and lilac for eyes add up to a make-up that perfectly complements an outrageous hairstyle.*

2: *Deep emerald shadow is skilfully brushed under the lids and round the eyes to highlight their rich hazel tones. Black liner softly frames the shape. Deep olive skin is shaped and shaded with rich, bronze blusher and toning lips.*

1

2

3: *Soft lips and cheeks leave the emphasis on strong eye make-up. Shades of rich, deep, royal blue blend into soft sky blue to echo the same colour accessories.*

4: *Stunning green eyes are given more prominence with a blend of bronze and copper shadows, rich burnt-orange lips and deliberately pale complexion.*

5: *A look that says 'fresh, young and healthy.' This girl's completely in the pink. Notice how everything about this make-up is soft save for the rather strong eyeliner shape? This look is reminiscent of the '50s' but right up to the minute for today's fashion trends.*

3

4

Chapter 5
Ten Years On

The years between early twenties and mid-thirties are an interesting time. Gone is the need to constantly experiment and many women tend to start to get into a rut make-up-wise. This should never really happen because it's just as important now as it always will be.

It's a sad fact, but true, that the ageing process really starts to get going even as early as the age of twenty-one or so. Of

2

1: *When Aimee walked into the studio, she was just a face in the crowd. With hair scraped away from a completely bare face she was pretty but hardly noticeable.*
2: *No, it is not a famous American pop singer, this is Aimee again, totally transformed. The full hairstyle accentuates her good bone structure and this is further helped by applying blusher right up to the temples. Suddenly, too, a pair of unremarkable eyes positively smoulder with clever shading and shaping.*

course this does vary from person to person but, from here on in it's a wise lady who pays extra special attention to skin care. As you get older, your skin starts to get dryer and elastin, the constituent that gives it it's ability to spring back, starts to cease its function. By your mid-thirties it's stopped working altogether so nothing short of plastic surgery will rid you of wrinkles. Far better to avoid them with regular moisturising; this will also give your skin vital protection against the elements.

It's doubtful that you will notice any changes overnight, but gradually, you may become aware that your skin doesn't have its usual suppleness. This signals the time for you to try new preparations: a slightly richer moisturiser, a cream foundation in favour of a lotion, cream or automatic eye shadows instead of loose powder and so on.

By now you will have a very good idea of the ideal shape you should be painting on your face and daily make-up will be much faster and simpler. If this is

1: Fiona has the perfect canvas for make-up although when we found her she was sporting a completely scrubbed complexion – a pity because she really needs to even up high colouring and accentuate her eyes.

2: As Fiona is really happiest with little or no make-up we devised this totally natural look for her that takes just a few minutes to copy. Pink colouring on cheeks disappears under green cover cream and a creamy beige foundation, brown kohl pencil gives shape at outer corners of eyes and mascara lengthens and beautifies her lashes. A soft peach blusher creates a healthy glow and soft coral lipstick keeps the look completely fresh and natural.

3: A dramatic evening blouse needs a

1

more theatrical look. Eyes are shaped with pale terracotta and frosted peach and shaded with brown kohl pencil. Soft amber blusher gives extra definition and a very pale frosted lipstick, outlined in deep pink, gives extra shape and excitement.

4: This make-up takes the transformation of Fiona one stage further, giving her an extra special polish with a look that wouldn't be out of place in the pages of a magazine. Burnt copper shimmer shadow highlights under the brow line. A rich deep blue shadow is brushed just above the crease line and under lower lids with a soft gold highlighting upper lids at the centre to give eyes an extra sparkle. Because her eyes have a much stronger look, Fiona's lips are painted in a dramatic burnt orange with blusher strengthened too to complete the effect.

2

3

the case, then you're an ideal candidate for falling into that rut, producing the same old face and colours every day.

A great way to avoid this little pitfall is to open your cosmetic drawer, arm yourself with cleansing lotion and tissues and shut the door on the world for an hour or so while you try out some colours and shapes to transform yourself once again. Most cosmetics will last for quite a long time and it's very rare that anyone actually uses up any eye shadow, blusher or lipstick completely and doesn't have a store of half used products lying around somewhere, ready for just this eventuality.

1: *Lesley is a good looking young housewife who tends to use lack of time as a reason for her clean, scrubbed look. She's blessed with stunning turquoise eyes, a clear complexion and beautiful, flowing blond hair.*

2: *This daytime look has been kept deliberately soft and very simple. A blend of khaki and beige shapes her eyes, bringing out their natural colour and soft coral blusher and lipstick give gentle emphasis.*

3: *This look graphically shows how easy it is to obtain a totally dated and very wrong look with cosmetics. False lashes, unless your natural ones are very short indeed, look positively 1950's. Blusher and highlighter have been applied in ugly, straight lines with no thought paid to careful blending and crimson lips are far too bright and harsh for a blonde.*

4: *Lesley wanted to try out a slightly different idea for an evening make-up.*

Here, blusher has been used not only to shape but also in place of eye shadow. A pale frosted brown has been used at outer corners to give eyes dimension and very fine false lashes add a touch of glamour. Lip colour for night time is stronger and tones beautifully with the overall pink effect of this make-up.

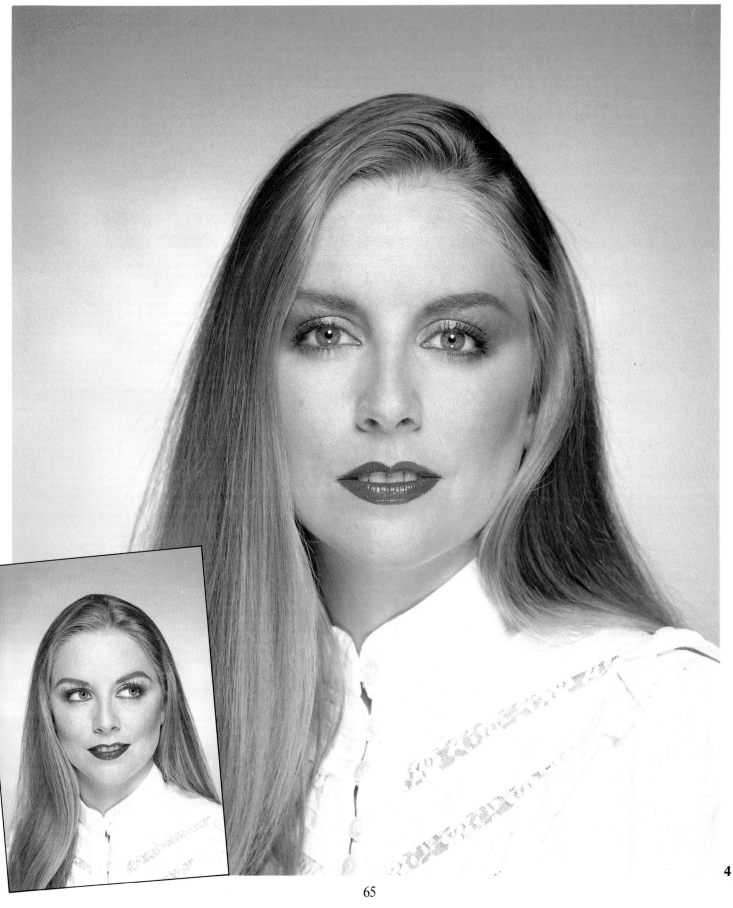

1: Catherine has a problem shared by many dark skinned people – uneven skin pigmentation. This is clearly visible here – she has light patches on cheeks, dark areas around her eyes and characteristic brown spots on her nose.

2: Here, her make-up, although expertly applied, emphasises the uneven colouring and makes her eyes seem heavier and slightly hooded.

3: A shade of cake foundation a touch lighter than her darkest tones and a shade darker than her lightest tones provides an ideal covering base for a more subtle make-up.

With Catherine's deep skin colouring, she can afford to be adventurous with her choice of eye shades: this brilliant combination of iridescent blue and mauve looks stunning. Because she has such prominent eyes, liquid liner can draw a defined line without looking harsh and unnatural. Blusher is applied high on cheek bones to further underline the importance of the eye make-up.

4: Dark skinned girls can wear pink and blue for a striking effect. Here rich frosted shades of midnight blue and petrol create beautiful eyes. Lip, cheek and nail colours co-ordinate perfectly to add to an exciting outdoors look.

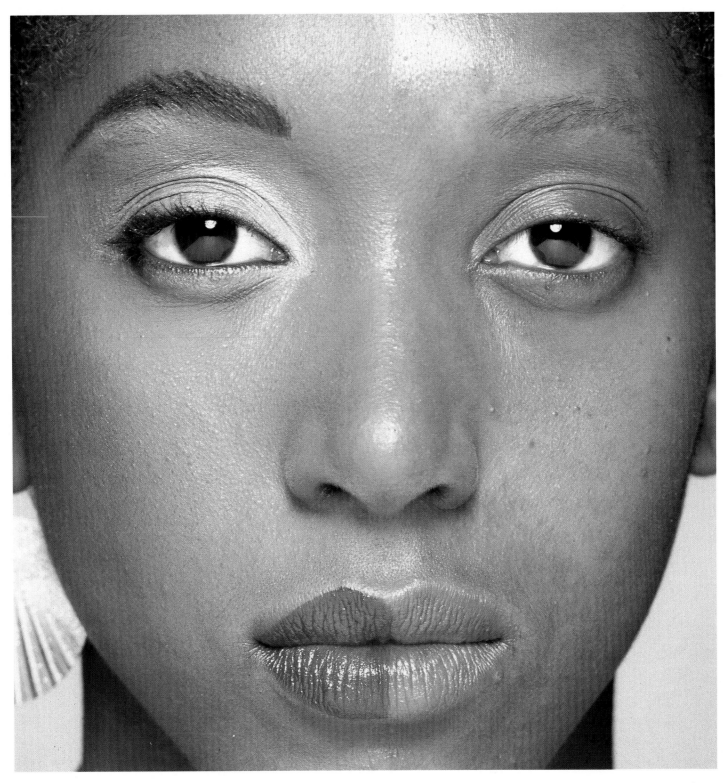

No, this isn't the latest in punk make-up! It's our way of showing very graphically how make-up has worked to bring out the best and hide the problems. Note how foundation has obliterated minor blemishes, dark down on upper lip and over-shiny skin. Blusher slims down chubby cheeks, lipstick hides uneven lip colouring, eyebrow pencil creates a frame for shimmering eye shades.

The finished look demonstrates how black girls can happily get away with really strong eye colour. Notice too how blusher is carried round the eye and up to the temples? With this stark hairdo this trick slims and frames the face perfectly.

1: *A very understated make-up creates a 'poor little rich girl' look. With hair casually brushed away from the face, careful attention has been paid to shape with light shading in shades of pink.*

2: *If you've got beautiful shaped lips then flaunt them. Strawberry blonde hair, coupled with yellow and amber accessories, dictate toning face shades made dramatic with brilliant orange lips.*

3: *A soft and simple daytime make-up is made instantly into an evening look with rich toffee shaded lips, carefully outlined to improve their shape.*

4: *Not every girl can be as adventurous as this. Golden shadow highlights under the brow line and a combination of copper and brown kohl shape the eyes. Classic high cheek bones are sculptured with pale golden frosted highlighter and rich peach shader. Soft, golden coral glossy lips add the perfect finishing touch.*

1

2 3 4

1: *Softly tanned skins on a warm summer evening need little to add a touch of beauty. Eyes are simply shaded and shaped with black kohl pencil, shine is toned down with translucent powder* and lips are given a touch of colour with brilliant pink.

2: *Use of colour has been deliberately played down here with shades to tone* with an olive complexion. Eyes are emphasised with shadows blending from black through to pale silver. Smoky pink lips complete a totally co-ordinated look.

Summer tanned skin needs very little or no make-up at all especially when you're young. Over the next two pages you'll find a montage of photographs of the same girl enjoying the sunshine with little more than a wardrobe of glossy lipsticks, kohl pencil and waterproof mascara. The looks are stunning, fresh and wholesome but could be ruined by strap marks, and burnt patches. Her most important holiday accessory therefore is her sunscreen that ensures even, light tanning without pain.

Chapter 6

Maturing Gracefully

Just because the age of forty has gone by it doesn't mean that you're over the hill. Far from it. In fact the mature woman is very much in fashion.

You have only to look as far as the film industry to see just how popular the forty-pluses are. Jane Fonda, Sophia Loren, Brigitte Bardot and even our own Joan Collins are all enjoying more success now that they have seen the last of their thirties. Perhaps one of the reasons for this is that maturity tends to bring a more relaxed outlook. Life isn't quite so frantic and fraught because age brings an ability to be more philosophical and you're less likely to let major problems upset you as much as fifteen years ago. Many women are fast discovering that this calmer attitude to life makes it a happier and more fulfilling time than any other age group.

1: *Alison, a bright, happy lady, agreed to let us photograph her without make-up to show graphically how lack of cosmetics can add years to a face. Her fine complexion is now marred by broken veins and laughter lines are emphasised without camouflage.*

1

2: *After applying green colour corrector, a base of warm beige gives subtle colour without looking unnatural. A soft turquoise cream shadow – which suits dry skin – follows the shape of her eye and only a single coat of mascara is needed to enhance lashes. Soft apricot lips and toning blusher give colour without looking harsh. The finished result takes at least ten years away from Alison's age, without looking like mutton done up as lamb, and it should take no more than six minutes to complete.*

3: *For a fast change into an evening look, blush and lip shades remain the same. To give an extra touch of glamour, Alison has chosen a frosted sable shade blended with her blusher to shape her eyes. Note too that she has cleverly hidden characteristic neck wrinkles with a pretty pearl choker.*

2

3

Now, just because the children have grown up and flown the nest there are no excuses for sitting back and becoming a frump. Instead it is time to adapt your beauty routine, complement the advance of time and make the most of it.

Basic skin care is of the utmost importance now, even if you have always been blessed with a trouble free complexion, it's almost certainly starting to get very dry indeed.

Fast losing the suppleness of youth, it will desperately need daily and nightly moisturising with rich lotions or creams to help redress the balance. Another danger area is eyelids which could show a tendency to become crepey, making shadow application more difficult. Use of a good eye cream does help to reduce the risk of this happening in the first place but avoiding the use of bright colours will help reduce its visibility too. In fact, subtlety is the watchword for make-up now. Soft, muted colours are far more flattering and far less ageing.

2

1

1: *Slim and attractive with lovely dark auburn hair and green eyes, Annabella has the potential to be a very elegant and good looking lady.*

2: *For her daytime look we chose soft and subtle shades of pink to suit her*

English Rose looks. Eyes are emphasised with a line of soft brown kohl pencil and delicately shadowed with a matte pale orchid. Rose pink blusher and lips colour blend beautifully.

3: *For a quick five minute change to an evening look, we kept the same basic*

make-up. Dark brown pencil is added for strength and silver grey shadow is brushed over lids and winged upwards. Blusher in the same shade as before is strengthened and lips are given a coat of a richer pink with a slick of gloss on top.

1: *Iris, seen here without her make-up, has beautiful blue eyes and a very good bone structure. She really should wear make-up to hide those broken veins and take away a few years.*

2: *This make-up achieves nothing. Bright blue shadow and strong dark lines look positively hard and ugly. A light covering of powder does nothing to disguise those broken veins and dark red lipstick is far too harsh for Iris's colouring.*

3: *Iris now looks ten years younger with this softer make-up. Pearly grey shadow and brown pencil really bring out the colour of her eyes. Uneven colouring is hidden under green cover cream and a warm beige foundation. A peach blusher gives warmth and pinky-beige lipstick completes the softening effect.*

1: *We met Sharron (left) spending a happy Mediterranean holiday with her family. It may be hard to believe but Sharman (right) is her fourteen year old daughter!*

Sharron is a very pretty lady who, like many with fair complexions, tends to redden a little in the sun. Had we met her before, we would have suggested a higher protection sunscreen on her face in order to avoid this happening. Instead, we designed this informal, easy to copy natural holiday make-up.

2: *A deep golden beige foundation gives a soft glow to sunburnt skin. Eyes are simply enhanced with dark charcoal grey kohl pencil drawn all around and brushed upwards at outer corners. Liberal application of brownish black waterproof mascara is guaranteed to stay put even on the hottest of nights. Amber blusher, lightly applied under cheek bones and soft rose lips completed Sharron's soft, young, summer evening make-up.*

Below *Eve is one of those rare and lucky women who can really look good without a stitch of make-up. She has a lovely, fresh complexion, sparkling eyes and a dazzling smile and very pretty elfin-like face. Here she is sporting just the very barest of essentials in natural toning shades.*

1: *Here's a perfect example of make-up co-ordinating with an outfit – every colour in Eve's evening blouse is mirrored in her face. Charcoal shadow on her eyes is covered with beautiful gold glitter and a yellow-gold powder shadow is used with dramatic effect as highlighter on cheek bones and at temples. Brilliant pink blusher isn't just reserved for cheeks either, it's used to give more emphasis to Eve's smooth and wrinkle-free forehead. Deep peach lipstick is just a perfect match to her blouse.*

2: *For an alternative glamorous evening, a soft khaki shadow blends perfectly into a rosy blusher which is swept from the eyelids up to her temples. The complete effect of this make-up gives Eve real style.*

Seasonal Changes

Just as you climb out of your winter woollies at the first warm breath of spring, so too should you switch your make-up. This should not just suit your outfit but also the light – cold, grey winter days demand a heavier make-up, whereas lighter, brighter spring and summer days dictate a far more natural look.

1 and 2: *Honey-tanned skin needs little or no make-up. Soft bronze blusher to shape, perhaps a rich deep red lipstick or just lip gloss and a soft pencil outline round the eyes for extra sparkle.*

2

3: *As summer tans fade and days become grey and miserable, put some warmth into your make-up with rich shades of burgundy and copper.*

4: *Winter heralds the start of the party season and a chance to wear glamorous glittery outfits and create an exciting new look with heavy eyes, pale and interesting complexion and startling lip shades.*

3

4

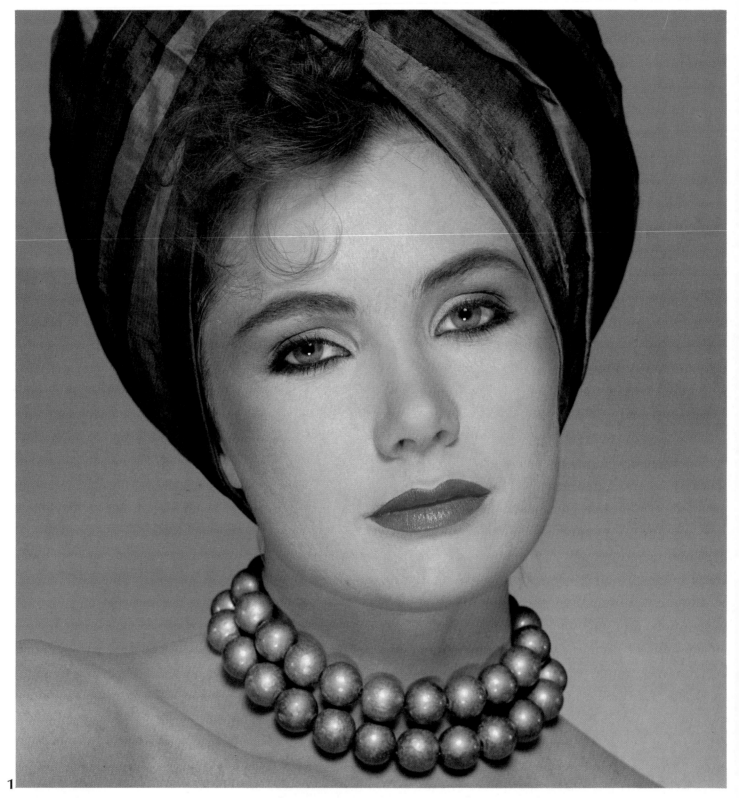

Same girl but two completely different looks for very special occasions.

1: *Here brilliant shades of green and gold cleverly echo the shades in Debra's choker necklace.*

2: *This stunning evening blouse needs a spectacular make-up to complement it.*

Eyes are shaped with silver and charcoal and given extra dimension with pink blusher applied under the brow line and

right up to her nose to slim and shape. Lips are painted a pale candy pink in order to leave full emphasis on the eyes.

Fantasy Faces *Fancy dress parties can often give you the ideal excuse for creating your own unique fantasy face. In fact, you can save yourself quite a bit of money by making your face the actual fancy dress.*

1: Just a Pussycat *A mane of strawberry blonde hair coupled with a fox scarf can make you the most glamorous lion at the party. This incredible make-up was drawn with charcoal and black and white eyepencils. It took over an hour to do but it's a real work of art.*

3

4

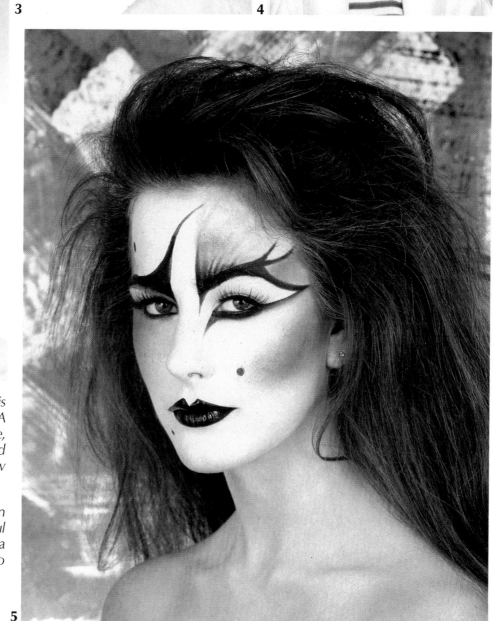

2

3: Pure Fantasy *This beautiful look is entitled 'Midsummer Nights Dream.' A soft ivory foundation forms the base, charcoal pencil provides the outline and pink and lilac pressed powder shadow create the subtle shading.*

5: Be a witch *This stunning creation instantly turns you into a rather beautiful witch: team it with a long black dress and a broomstick and there you are ready to bewitch all at the party.*

5

95

8
An Introduction to Haircare

A new hairstyle is a great morale booster. That marvellous natural fibre, hair, can make you feel on top of the world, or plunge you into the depths of despair. Your hair can change your appearance and mood dramatically, and in a way it is the cheapest form of cosmetic surgery you are ever likely to undergo.

Throughout history hairstyles have reflected the trends in fashion and the economic climate. In some cases, the importance of a person was instantly recognisable from the hairstyle he or she wore. Luckily, your hairstyle no longer has to indicate your social standing, but as a fashion accessory it is without parallel.

All of us become frustrated with our hair at times – when it refuses to obey, or curl the way we want it to. Bedrooms should be re-classified as DANGER ZONES, where grips, pins and heated rollers fly heavenward, and the air turns blue. In fact, the man in your life interrupts at his peril with the suggestion that you "Get a move on", and seriously risks mortal injury from a flying tail comb.

As you struggle valiantly with your wayward locks, your escort, by now relegated to the hall, waits patiently for you to appear. Finally, you materialise. A vision of beauty? No, your temper is frayed, you feel a mess no matter what you put on, and you wish like mad that you didn't have to go out.

Sounds familiar? It should, after all who hasn't shed a few tears over a disastrous hairdo?

This book has been produced with all such problems in mind. Hopefully, some of the ideas on the following pages will help to restore your equilibrium, rescue ailing friendships and result in a beautiful "Crowning Glory".

There are conditioners to suit every type and texture of hair. Try one to keep your hair looking good and feeling great.

9
You and Your Hair

Are you completely happy with your hair? What woman is? Either your hair is too straight, too curly (didn't you just hate it, when as a child every relative said, "What pretty curls you have"), too fine, too thick, dark brown when you long to be an ice-cool blonde or vice versa. In fact, in a perverse way we always want the opposite of what we have got.

Hairdressers and hair care manufacturers have kept pace with the demands of the modern woman, and now virtually anyone with straight hair can go curly, and literally any colour under the sun is possible, from subtle chestnut to fuchsia pink. But before we get carried away with thoughts of bouncy curls or raven-haired locks, let's take a look at your hair in its natural state, and see what you can do to improve it.

Working From The Inside Out.

Over the last few years a great deal has been written about the importance of a healthy diet and regular exercise. Indeed, hardly a month goes by without one of the popular women's magazines bringing to our attention just how unfit we all are. These days it is impossible to avoid the fact that a balanced diet and exercise not only help you to maintain a healthy body internally, but also keep those outward signs of good health: clear skin, bright eyes, strong nails and glossy, bouncy hair, in tip-top condition.

Eyes, skin, nails and hair are perfect indicators of how well we are functioning. If you are feeling a little off colour, your skin begins to look pale and sallow; the eyes become dull and lose their sparkle; nails suddenly start to flake and your hair lacks lustre, becoming limp and lifeless. We have all looked in a mirror when we have felt under the weather, and seen these signs for ourselves. Obviously this indicates that

1. *Sue is fortunate enough to have easy-to-control, medium-textured hair, with plenty of natural bounce. But the overgrown shape leaves a lot to be desired.*
2. *With this type and texture of hair your choice of style is wide and varied. Sue opted for a similar but shorter shape which she can manage easily herself.*

3

3. *After a strenuous workout don't reach for that chocolate bar, a fresh crunchy carrot . . .*

4

4. *. . . or a crisp stick of celery will appease your hunger and help keep you fit.*

what goes on inside is soon reflected on the outside, and logically, a poor diet which does not give the body all the nutrients it needs to function properly, will soon take its toll on our hair and skin.

How can diet affect your hair? Once your hair appears above the surface of the scalp it is already dead, so it's beneath the skin that all the action takes place. The indentation in the skin from which hair protrudes is called the hair follicle, and at the base of the follicle is a minute nodule called the papilla. Very simply, the papilla is like a small factory, producing and feeding the cells which form our hair. So, even if you do accidentally pull out some of your hair by the roots, providing the papilla is still functioning the hair will grow again. For our small factory to work properly it needs an efficient blood supply, which in turn carries the basic requirements to ensure continued factory production – digested protein (amino-acids). Stop supplying the basic raw material and, like any factory, it will slowly stop producing and eventually grind to a halt.

1

This does not mean that you have to live on a diet of pure protein for your hair's sake. In fact, this would be extremely bad for you. Simply ensure that you have a healthy diet – plenty of fresh fruit, lean meat, vegetables and salads. High-grade proteins such as fish, eggs, cheese, milk and meat are

particularly beneficial, as they are rich in the nitrogen and sulphur essential for healthy hair growth. Avoid too many sweets, chocolates, cakes and biscuits, and beware of being too heavy-handed with animal fats. Drink plenty of water, at

1. *Long and lustrous – the visual image that epitomises healthy hair.*
2. *Fine hair is a problem that many of us share with Tracey. As you can see it soon looks untidy when the layers are allowed to grow long and straggly.*
3. *Cutting the sides and back short removes the untidy layers, and is an ideal style for fine, thin hair.*

3

4. *Very curly, coarse hair has a tendency to be dry, fragile and unruly. Dawn is well aware of her hair problems and its limitations.*

5. *To grow hair of this texture long, requires care and patience. But whether you wear your hair long or short, daily applications of moisturiser and regular conditioning treatments are a must.*

5

least six glasses a day to clear your system, and remember to include some wholewheat cereal, bread or bran in your diet to supply the necessary fibre content.

If the thought of exercise makes you groan, then just think of the good it will do you. Working out to music can be fun. Pretend you are auditioning for a dance group such as 'Hot Gossip', rather than doing repetitive, boring physical jerks, and enjoy yourself. Remember as you leap around, that your oxygen intake is increased, your pulse rate raised, and your circulation stimulated. An efficient circulation means that every part of your body is being well-supplied with blood; this includes the blood vessels (capillaries) which supply the papilla with its raw material: digested protein.

Now we come to a very important point; learn to relax. Tension and nervous strain not only make you irritable, even ill at times, but can also bring about disorders of the hair and scalp. I know it is not easy in this day and age, but try to pace yourself, organise your day, and count to ten when you feel the pressure building up. Incidentally, exercise is a marvellous way of working off nervous energy and clearing the mind.

Having dealt with the way you can help your hair from the inside, we can now concentrate on the part which is visible; the hair shaft.

Every strand of hair consists of three basic layers. The outer layer is called the cuticle, and plays an important part in how our hair looks and feels. This layer could be compared to the scales of a fish.

It consists of a series of overlapping scales, which may be up to seven layers in thickness. The cuticle protects the second layer or cortex; here we find nearly all our natural colour pigment, melanin. It is this layer which provides the hair with its strength, texture and elasticity. In fact, curling and all types of hairstyling depend on temporary alterations to the structure of the cortex. In the centre is the medulla; the function of the medulla is unknown, and in some cases it is missing altogether. But don't worry whether you have a medulla or not because the hair does not seem to suffer without it.

On average we have 90,000 to 140,000 strands of hair on our heads. Naturally blond people have slightly more than brunettes, and the people

1. *Slim, attractive eighteen-year-old Sarah requires a style that will place more emphasis on her eyes and mouth, and truly reflect her lively personality.*
2. *A perm adds body and the cut – a pretty layered bob enhances the eyes and that lovely smile. A simple scrunch dry ensures that Sarah will be able to manage her new style.*

with lower than average hair density are usually the red-heads. Paradoxically, red-heads often look as though they have thick hair because it tends to be of a coarser texture, whilst blondes will have fine hair, which can look limp and thin.

This brings us neatly to texture and density, two terms which are often confused. Texture generally refers to the quality of one single strand, and density to the amount of hair on your head. These two terms are very important to you when deciding on a new hairstyle.

Fine hair tends to be soft and fly-away; if it is thin as well then another problem is added. Shorter styles usually work best, and a soft perm will add body giving the appearance of thicker hair. Fine, thick (dense) hair can be grown longer and works well when cut into short or long bob lines.

If your hair is fine but naturally curly, then use the curl as much as possible. Curly styles are so attractive that it is a shame to spend time and money creating a sleek style.

Medium-textured hair is very versatile, responding well to perming, setting and blow-drying. Virtually any style is suitable, depending on your physical characteristics.

Coarse hair often looks thick and heavy – think of red-heads or oriental girls. Sharp, geometric cuts can look superb but if your hair is on the thin side, stick to reasonably short styles. Naturally curly, coarse hair is inclined to have a will of its own and needs careful cutting to prevent it from looking bushy and unruly.

By now you should have a good idea as to the quality and texture of your hair. Sit down in front of a mirror and try to be really objective. Do you have masses of

hair or is it only wishful thinking? If a single strand of hair feels like a pure silk thread then it is probably fine-textured. If, on the other hand, it feels more like a strand of cotton then it means you are blessed

with coarse hair. Medium-textured hair falls somewhere in-between. Having assessed your hair you should try to accept it, along with all its limitations. Learn to be happy with what nature has given you and work with it rather than against it.

As mentioned earlier, hairdressers and manufacturers can work wonders, combining good products and expert skill, but it's your understanding of the basic raw material that makes all the difference.

One interesting fact that proves just how individual we all are, is the use of hair in crime detection. Some experts claim that a strand of hair from a suspect, when subjected to certain tests, can identify

individual characteristics, including age, sex, blood group, illnesses and drug use. So when you hear the phrase, "No two heads are alike", you'll know that it really is true.

10
Choosing a New Hairstyle

I often find it interesting to go to a social gathering, where my profession is unknown, and simply listen to the people talking. It's amazing what you can learn about your own business. Conversations vary but eventually, after the compliments about clothes and how well everybody is looking subside, the topic often turns to hair. Comments such as: "I simply can't get a decent haircut" or "My perm went straight after six weeks", are fairly common. Some people will delve into the depths of their handbags and produce pictures of svelte, golden-haired beauties who can't weigh more than seven and a half stone. They then proceed to criticise their hairdressers for not sending them out of

3. Paula has a lovely oval face which can take virtually any hairstyle. As a model she finds her long hair very useful because of its versatility.

4. A very similar style to Wendy's (overleaf) but far more severe. The sleek sides accentuate her oval face, while the curls add an air of femininity.

4

the salon, a carbon copy of the girl in the photo. After several more statements like these my conscience begins to prick and I have to own up to being a hairdresser, even though I know that for the rest of the evening I will be inundated with questions about hair.

Two of the most common subjects people talk to me about are: not being able to find the right hairdresser, and the desire to look like someone else (just like my new friends with their carefully preserved pictures). Let us take a closer look at the second point first.

We all present a different image. Some people are always elegant and chic, others smart but casual. The majority of us like to ring the changes – smart for business; casual during leisure time; sophisticated or *avant-garde* for evenings. Putting your "Total Image" together requires just a little common sense and self-awareness. Above all, don't try to be a carbon copy of someone else – be yourself, with your own sense of style.

"Total Image" includes many factors:
  1. Height.
  2. Your size.
  3. The way you dress
    (the majority of
    the time).
  4. Occupation.
  5. Life-style.
  6. Personality.

Points One And Two. Your hair should be balanced; in proportion with the rest of your body. For example, if you are five feet tall and weigh sixteen stone, a short crop is going to make you look like a triangle. If you are tall then you do not need a high hairstyle. It would only accentuate your height.

Points Three And Four. The way you dress the majority of the time, often depends on your occupation. If you have to be conservative in your dress, then your hair should be smart and neat. As your dress becomes more flamboyant, so can your hairstyle.

Point Five. Most of us lead hectic lives, whether it's being a busy mum, sales assistant or secretary. So if time is of the essence, make sure that a new hairstyle isn't going to demand more time and effort than you are prepared to give to keep it looking good.

Point Six. If you are an extrovert by nature you're probably more willing to try out new styles regularly. Shy, introverted people tend to stick with the same hairstyle, taking far longer to decide on a change. For the introverted person a new hairstyle can work wonders. It's amazing how a different appearance can boost the ego and give confidence. Or you may be like me and not fit into any single category. You may be an extrovert or an introvert, depending on the situation and how relaxed you feel with the people around you. The same applies to clothes. One day you may wear classic skirts and sweaters, the next day jump-suits and camouflage jackets. If this is your predicament then the hairstyle you choose must be adaptable, so that you can change your image at will.

"Total Image" is important. The girls you see in magazines have it – that is why they look so good. Everything in a photograph is worked out to the last detail, right down to the colour of the model's nail polish. Try to remember this when you are creating an image, however temporary, and that your hair is as vital to that finished look as clothes, make-up and accessories.

"That's all very well," I can hear you saying to yourself, 'my image is fine, but what about my hair and face?" Right, first of all your face-shape. Certain basic principles normally apply when determining the shape of a hairstyle in relation to the face.

A round face requires fullness on the top and crown, with the hair dressed close to the face at the sides to reduce width.

A long face requires very little height; fullness at the sides and if applicable a soft fringe to reduce a high forehead.

With a square face, hair should be dressed fuller on the sides and top; closer at the temples and lower jawline to soften squareness.

An oval face is generally considered the perfect face-shape; it requires little corrective styling.

In most cases these rules apply but as the saying goes, "Rules are made to be broken". The modern woman's approach to make-up enables her to alter her face-shape at will by skilful application of shaders, blushers and highlighters. These illusions, created with make-up, allow us the freedom to try out more varied and daring hairstyles.

Once again study yourself in a mirror, this time looking for your good features. Pull your hair back and look straight into the mirror, and then using a hand-mirror, turn and look at your profile. Eyes, nose, cheekbones, jawline, mouth; decide which particular aspect of your face you like best, then let your hair go. If the one thing you liked about your face no longer looks as good as it did then your hairstyle is wrong.

A good style will emphasise your best features, drawing the eye towards them. This automatically detracts from your less-than-perfect points, thus minimising them.

Your hairstyle completes your total image and should be in harmony with your clothes, in proportion with your body, and emphasise you best facial features.

Now that you know a little more about your hair and its importance as a fashion accessory, we have to go in search of a hairdresser who can understand you as well as you understand yourself.

Trying to find a new hairdresser can be a traumatic experience. You may be lucky and already have a regular hairdresser who fulfils your requirements, but if you're still looking, here are a few tips to smooth the path to the salon door. If the salon was recommended by a friend, look at her hair. Does it impress you? Do you admire her well-groomed and up-to-date looks? Do you have similar tastes? If the answer to all three questions is yes, then the salon could be worth a visit.

Perhaps you have seen a salon's

Choosing a New Hairstyle

1. Happy with her hair the length and shape it is, Wendy wanted a temporary change of image. Preferably a style that she could recreate at home for a special occasion.

2. Heated rollers to smooth the curl, a little backcombing and the longer hair pinned up leaving the ends and top in loose curls. Quick and easy; the type of style a busy housewife like Wendy appreciates.

Your first appointment in a new salon should be for a blow-dry or set. It is unwise to have a cut, perm or colour at this early stage. Give your new hairdresser a chance to get to know your **1**

2

hair. Don't expect miracles on your first visit. It may take several appointments before you are really happy with the style. After a few visits your hairdresser will have a good picture of your total image. By chatting to you he or she should have assessed your personality, your likes and dislikes. You may be surprised and pleased with the styles suggested. A new hairdresser will see you in a different light from family and old friends, who rarely suggest a change and

accept you as you are. Usually they are the first ones to compliment you on a new look, making you wonder what sort of wreck you looked like in the past. On your trip to any salon, look around. It should be very clean; the towels and gowns freshly laundered; the magazines current issues. Do the staff look smart and professional? Would you trust them with your precious locks if they didn't? When you're kept waiting, are you offered a cup of coffee as well as an

explanation as to the delay? Don't be satisfied with a dirty or inefficient salon. After all you are paying the bill. Finally, try to enjoy your visits to the salon. It's a time to relax and be pampered. Close your eyes. Forget the shopping, work and the kids and for a change just concentrate on yourself.

promotional pictures in the local paper. It's nice to see a salon that is proud of the work they produce and promotes its name accordingly, through the media. If the styles portrayed are your idea of good grooming, then possibly this is the salon for you.

It could be that you liked the look of the salon: maybe it was small and friendly, large and efficient, or ultra-modern with disco music wafting through the open door. Always choose a salon that you feel comfortable and relaxed in.

Once you have chosen the salon, try to make your appointment in person. This gives you the chance to see inside the shop and in some salons it is possible to have a consultation with your prospective stylist well in advance. This is the time you check the cost, before you start. Don't be embarrassed. We all have to watch the purse-strings these days. Make sure that everything you require is included in the price quoted. I have met so many people who have nearly had a fit when handed the final bill, and their bank managers have not appreciated an overdrawn account because of a new hairdo. For the cost conscious, many colleges that run hairdressing courses have salons which are open to the general public. The work is done by students under the guidance of an experienced tutor. Private schools also require models for beginners as well as advanced students. The cost in both instances is far lower than salon prices, so they may be the answer if money is tight. However, you must allow plenty of time when going to a school and be as flexible as possible in your style ideas. Good salons also run training sessions for staff and may require suitable models. Watch the local press and salon windows for advertisements.

11

Are Conditioners Important?

Hair is a marvellous natural fibre. We wash it, apply heat and chemicals to it, and generally abuse it. Could you imagine wearing a pure silk dress and putting it through the same rigorous treatment, every day, year in, year out? Of course not. So why doesn't hair deserve the same delicate care as that expensive silk dress? Well it does, which is why correct shampooing and conditioning are important. After all you can easily replace a dress but hair can't be bought.

You could be forgiven for getting confused when confronted with the massive array of shampoos and conditioners now available. Which one do you choose? One way round the problem is to ask your hairdresser, who may stock a special professional range which is retailed in the salon; you'll then be given advice on what to use and how and when. This is particularly useful if you have problem or chemically treated hair. Even if the salon does not carry a retail range, do ask your hairdresser for assistance. We all like to see you with your hair in good condition.

Shampoos. A modern shampoo is a cleanser, designed to remove everyday dirt, grime and grease without stripping the hair of its precious natural moisture content. Strong alkaline products which strip the hair, rob it of moisture which leaves it looking dull and lifeless. Hair has a natural acid mantle and this is why many shampoos are now acid-balanced to the hair; obviously these are better for you than something that is as strong as a biological washing powder. Additives are also included to condition the hair, making it easier to comb, and ingredients put in to improve certain problems such as static (fly-away hair), dryness, excessive grease and mild dandruff.

When your hair has been chemically treated, choose a mild shampoo designed for tinted or permed hair; one that does not strip out artificial colour or reduce permed hair to a dry frizz. If you have naturally dry hair, select a mild shampoo. The same also applies if you like to wash your hair frequently.

Greasy hair should be kept clean otherwise it soon looks flat and loses its bounce. Greasy hair also tends to attract dirt and grime, which can clog the follicles and cause more serious scalp problems.

Whether your hair is normal, dry or greasy, keep it clean. I am a great believer in shampooing as often as you feel it is necessary, although not just for the sake

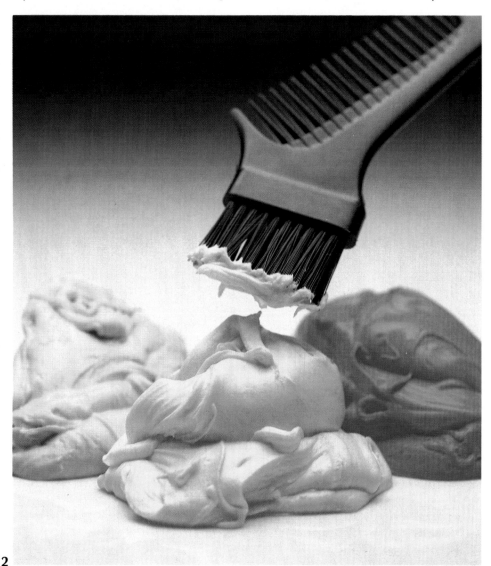

1. *We are not suggesting that you "wash that man right out of my hair"! On the contrary − clean, sweet-smelling hair makes you nice to be near.*
2. *Super conditioners that look almost good enough to eat.*

2

of it. A dirty or greasy scalp is the perfect breeding ground for bacteria, increases the risk of infection as well as making your hair smell extremely unpleasant.

Choosing the right shampoo is a matter of trial and error. Read the labels and select the one most suitable for your hair type. Always buy the smallest size at first, then if you do not like it your money has not literally "Gone down the drain". Colour, perfume and the shape of the bottle, have nothing to do with the quality of the product inside. They are selling points, dreamed up by the advertising and marketing people, to tempt you into buying their shampoo. A

1

other reasons the hair may also have lost some of its elasticity; an important ingredient for successful styling. Most surface acting conditioners contain lanolin, cholesterol, vegetable and mineral oils, and acetic or citric acids. Because they are mildly acidic they close the cuticle and coat the hair shaft, rather like a fabric conditioner, thereby protecting the delicate cortex from further damage and moisture loss. The elasticity is also improved by this closing and shrinking action. Since the cuticle scales are now tightly shut, the hair's visual appearance, lustre and manageability are greatly enhanced.

2

3

better guide is to take your hairdresser's advice, or to choose a well known brand name with a good reputation for hair cosmetics.

Conditioners. After shampooing, a mildly acidic rinse or conditioner should always be applied. As with shampoo, various types are available for greasy, dry, normal, permed, tinted or relaxed hair. How do they work? Cream rinses and

similar products are collectively termed surface acting conditioners. Being mildly acidic they work on the outer layer of the hair shaft: the cuticle. The cuticle, which you will remember is made up of overlapping scales, is the first part of the hair to suffer damage. When these imbrications are raised through general day to day wear and tear, your hair becomes tangly, dry, porous and dull. For

1. *Little did Cathy realise what she had let herself in for when she requested a treatment to moisturise and condition her dry hair.*
2. *Wax treatments with a difference – coloured to suit your mood, and, of course, condition your hair. Yellow – to brighten and lift your spirits.*
3. *Blue – for when you feel moody and romantic.*

4

Very dry, porous, brittle or chemically treated hair needs the more intensive treatment provided by a restructurant or protein pac. This type of deep acting conditioner comes in several forms: a coloured but transparent liquid; a light cream; or as a thick, heavy cream packed in individual treatment sachets. Sachets and bottles display clear reference as to the hair problem they are designed for. Do not expect instant results after just one treatment; if your hair is badly damaged it will take regular use of the product to show a maintained improvement. Just as a doctor never prescribes one antibiotic, but a whole course of tablets, so your hair will require a complete course and regular applications of restructurants/protein treatments. Containing hydrolysed protein and moisturizers with a similar molecular weight to that of the hair, these protein treatments penetrate through the cuticle into the cortex. Attracted to the damaged internal structure, the molecules form temporary bonds within the hair shaft, strengthening the hair and improving its texture.

4. *Blow-drying naturally curly hair like Jacqueline's, can be very drying and damaging, so remember to condition every time you shampoo.*

If you feel that you have a serious or worrying hair/scalp problem, do seek professional advice from your hairdresser or doctor. If they are unable to help then you will probably be recommended to a trichologist, who specialises in conditions of the hair and scalp.

The way in which you use these products is as important as the time you spend choosing them.

Shampooing And Conditioning Procedure. Before beginning, assemble everything you will need. Brush your hair thoroughly to remove tangles and loosen debris. Pour approximately two tablespoons of shampoo into a beaker and dilute it by adding a little warm water. Most shampoos are quite concentrated, and we all make the mistake of using far too much straight from the bottle.

Using a shower attachment, or one of the devices that can be fixed over the taps, wet your hair with warm water. Apply some of the diluted shampoo and massage through the hair to distribute it evenly.

Now give your scalp a firm massage, using the tips of the fingers, not the nails. With a circular motion work over the entire head several times, paying particular attention to the hairline where make-up collects.

Rinse very thoroughly and repeat the shampoo sequence as before. When you come to the final rinse, touch your hair: does it feel clean and free from shampoo? If in doubt continue rinsing. Wrap your hair 'turban style' in a clean towel.

A word of advice to those of you who shampoo every two or three days. Only one application of shampoo should be necessary and try not to over wash.

After shampooing, pat your hair dry with the towel to remove excess water, never rub.

Comb your hair through with a wide-toothed comb, working from ends to roots, gently removing any tangles.

Apply conditioner or protein treatment according to the directions. If you must comb through the conditioner then use the wide-toothed shampoo comb, and as before, work from ends to roots.

Leave on for the specified time and, prior to rinsing, gently massage the hair and scalp to loosen the product and aid in its removal.

Proceed with the final rinse, which may take slightly longer if the conditioner is very thick and heavy.

Now towel-blot and comb through as before.

When your hair is wet, only use a comb to remove tangles, one with wide evenly-spaced teeth and smooth rounded tips. Hair is very vulnerable when wet and extremely elastic. Using a brush to remove tangles, over-stretches and pulls the hair causing breakage and eventually unsightly split ends.

Treat your hair as gently as that expensive silk dress and the results will soon be evident.

12
Make it Last

If you have avoided using setting lotions in the past, fearing that they would give your hair a fixed, unnatural look, then think again. Today's setting lotions are more than just liquids which solidify the hair. They add body and gloss, control fly-away hair, and generally make it more manageable. Modern setting agents are a far cry from the gum-based lotions of yesteryear that held every wave and curl rigidly in place, irritated the scalp, and often flaked when dry, giving the appearance of permanent dandruff. Most of these problems have now been eliminated, and the range of products enlarged to allow for the variations in hair texture, condition and modern styling techniques.

Why use setting agents? The obvious reason is that they help to make your style last longer, but there are other advantages. Some of the spirit-based lotions actually help your hair to dry faster; others contain conditioners and anti-static properties, which, as previously mentioned, aid styling and control the hair more effectively. Many setting agents and sprays are also reversion resistant: this simply means that they protect the hair from absorbing moisture from the atmosphere, whether it's steam from hot water or just the damp of a humid day. I would emphasise the fact that they only help to protect, and if your surroundings are very damp or wet then do cover your head with a light scarf.

Setting agents come in several forms and a variety of containers such as **2** aerosol cans, bottles, tubes and jars.

----

1. *Hairsprays protect and prolong the life of your style, whether it is sleek or curly.*
2. *Foam goes much further than you think, so take care when you spray, or like our model you could end up with more than you bargained for.*

Which one you choose depends on your hair type and style.
Setting Lotions are available in either small individual bottles, containing enough lotion for one set, or large containers with sufficient for maybe ten or twelve applications, depending on the length and density of your hair.

You are now faced with the problem of which type and strength to select. For the majority of people I would recommend normal to light hold. These are quite strong enough for the average hair. However, if you find that you require something firmer then progress to the stronger extra hold.

1

2

3

When you have a particular problem, such as dry or greasy hair, choose a lotion which is formulated to combat the condition.

Setting lotions are applied to clean towel-dried hair after shampooing, prior to styling. Care should be taken not to empty the entire contents of the bottle onto the top of your head. Make sure that you sprinkle the lotion over all the hair ends, lengths, and roots. As you apply the lotion, work it through with your free hand, moving the top hair out of the way to ensure that the back and underneath hair gets its fair share. Finally comb through and set.

One useful tip from the professionals: if you use heat to dry your hair, wait until the set has cooled before removing the rollers. You will find that your hair has more bounce and that the style lasts longer.

Blow Dry Lotions are similar to setting lotions in that they add body, bounce, gloss and reduce static. They can also be purchased in individual or large economy bottles but there the similarity ends. If you have ever tried a setting lotion for blow-drying you will know how difficult it can be. As the hair begins to dry the brush gets stuck, tangles form, and what should be a gentle process of manipulating the brush through the hair, whilst applying warm air, becomes a

tortuous procedure, hard on your temper and very hard on your hair. Blow dry lotions are normally available in one strength only, as they are designed for more natural, softer styles, not a firm set. Apply as you would a setting lotion to clean, towel-dried hair.

Quick Set Sprays are ideal for refreshing your style between shampoos. Packaged in aerosol cans, they are quick and simple to use. There is no need to wet the hair or purchase heated rollers. Brush your hair through and part the first section to be rolled; spray sparingly and wind the hair around the roller. Continue over the entire head spraying each rollered section. Wait approximately ten minutes then remove the rollers and brush through.

The sprays are a marvellous standby for when that unexpected invitation crops up. No need to use that old excuse "But I'm washing my hair tonight", unless you want to that is!

Gels have truly come into their own during the Seventies and Eighties. Resurrected by the professional hairdresser, and reformulated to suit today's styles, gels can be used to achieve a variety of looks for blow-drys and sets to more high fashion *avant-garde* designs. The trick is in how much to use. Available in tubes or jars, the gel is translucent and similar in consistency to

1. *Even very short hairstyles require support. Spread a little gel onto your fingers . . .*
2. *. . . and massage it through your hair, paying particular attention to the root area, and then dry into shape.*
3. *Although Ruth's hair is fine and thin the gel adds enough body to keep the top full and feathery.*

a partially set jelly. For blow-drying and setting, a small amount is massaged through freshly shampooed, towel-dried hair. For slick wet-look styles, apply more gel, comb the hair into shape and leave to dry. Do not brush through or the wet-look effect will be lost. If you favour a voluminous, spiky shape, blow or finger dry your hair using gel, particularly at the roots, to give body and volume. When the style is complete, apply gel to the tips of the hair, with your fingers, and leave to dry. Gel containing glitter and colour is now available, so for more exciting styles turn to the chapter entitled "Dazzling Display".

Mousse – the name speaks for itself, is packaged in an aerosol can and resembles shaving foam or whipped cream when applied. It is currently the top styling aid for professional and home use. Whether you have a wash and wear permed look or a traditional set, mousse is the ideal setting agent, adding volume and conditioning the hair as well as protecting it from the effects of blow-drying and direct heat.

Apply to clean, damp hair. Simply squirt some of the mousse into the palms of your hands and massage through. It may take a little practice before you know exactly how much to use so start by following the directions on the can and gradually increase the amount if your style is not full or firm enough.

Gel and mousse can be purchased from hairdressing salons, or some of the larger chemists.

4

5

Hair Sprays protect your hairstyle from the elements whilst allowing it to move and still look natural. Gone are the hard lacquers that turned white and powdery, required special lacquer removing shampoos, and made you feel as if you were wearing a helmet on your head. During the Fifties and Sixties the *bouffant*, beehive styles led to the overuse and misuse of lacquers. People still remember their dry, brittle, broken hair and are wary of using anything to protect their styles. But modern sprays are different, lighter and water-soluble. They are easily removed by brushing and shampooing.

When purchasing, choose a can which states hair spray and not hair lacquer. To apply, hold the can approximately ten to twelve inches from your hair, and keep the can moving as you spray. There should be no need to plaster your hair. If the style does not stay in place try a firmer, extra hold spray.

If you use any form of setting agent or hair spray, do make sure that you brush your hair thoroughly at night.

Once setting lotions, gels or mousses have been used, the style can be boosted by putting rollers in before a shower or warm bath. Or in the case of a full, natural look, slightly dampen the hair

4. *Spray an orange-sized amount of foam into your hands, more if your hair is longer, and massage it through your hair.*
5. *As you can see, Susie's scrunch dried hair has plenty of volume. By varying the amount you use, foam is perfect for setting, blow, scrunch or finger drying.*

and lift it with your fingers until dry. The moisture helps to reactivate the setting agent.

All of these products help to keep your hair looking well-groomed, and the few extra pence they cost per application are well-invested when you consider that they "Make It Last".

13
Up-dated Setting

Believe it or not, many people do prefer to set their hair. In some cases this means setting on rollers after every shampoo; in others only occasionally when a temporary change is required. Maybe you prefer curly to straight hair or vice versa, and a perm for various reasons is

1. *Josanne's very straight hair is to be waved and curled using a technique which will be more familiar to our grandmothers – marcel waving.*

2. *Marcel waving such long hair is a time-consuming process, but we thought you would like to see how the old technique can be adapted to produce an ultra-feminine style.*

out of the question. Or perhaps you desire to create a different image for a special night out. Whatever the reason, setting is an ideal way to experiment with new looks.

First, let us take a look at the equipment you will need.

Rollers should be smooth with no

brushes or spikes as they only damage your hair.

Pins to secure the rollers; preferably plastic rather than metal, which can scratch the scalp.

Pincurl clips for stray ends and curls.

Some tissue cut into small oblongs.

Scotch tape.

119

Large styling comb and tail comb.

Hair brushes, which can be natural bristle, plastic or a combination of both. The bristles should be fairly widely spaced to penetrate through your hair. With plastic, each quill must be smooth, rounded at the tip and well-finished.

Having shampooed your hair and applied a setting lotion, gel or mousse, picture in your mind the finished style and comb the wet hair into a similar pattern.

Begin at the front and pick up with the end of your tail comb a small section of hair the same size as your roller. Comb it out from the head, slightly over the top of the section; wrap the ends in a small **1**

sections together. Place the hair in its final position either with a comb or your fingers. If the result of your set is too much curl, soften with more brushing, or use a blow-dryer, allowing the cool air to flow through the hair for a second or two until a softer curl is achieved. Finish off with a light coating of hairspray.

To set the style using heated rollers, brush your hair thoroughly and then follow the same procedure as for wet setting. Protecting the ends of your hair with tissue is now a must; heated rollers can be very drying and damaging, especially if your hair is fairly long. Treat these rollers as a stand-by to boost or quickly change your style. For the sake of

1. *Shaggy hair like Kay's that needs taming, or flat hair that requires lift, will respond well to setting on heated rollers.*
2. *Prepare your hair first by brushing it thoroughly to remove any tangles.*
3. *Kay preferred to set her longer back hair first, although you would normally begin*

at the front. Remember to protect the ends with tissue before putting in the roller.
4. *Finally the shorter front hair is rolled back and slightly to one side. Wait for the rollers to cool, then remove them and brush through.*

5. *Now that the hair is smooth it can be dressed into a more sophisticated style. The long back hair is swept up into a ponytail and gripped firmly at the crown.*
6. *Backcomb the front and smooth over to the side and back. Grip any long stray ends close to the ponytail. Using a hairpin,*

---

piece of tissue. This prevents frizzy and buckled ends.

Place the protected ends around the roller and wind down to the scalp. Secure with a pin.

Continue in this manner over the entire head, following the wet pattern you created.

Shorter hair may need pin-curling; take a small mesh, roll the hair up like a

Catherine Wheel from the ends back towards the scalp, and hold in place with a pincurl clip.

Stray ends can be positioned and held in place with Scotch tape. For a more wild, wavy look, twist each section of hair before putting in the roller.

When the hair is completely dry and cool, remove the rollers. Brush through to relax the curl, and blend the roller

your hair try not to use them every day.

Curling tongs and hot brushes, what did we do without them? Handy to carry about, perfect for holidays or just perking up your style. As with heated rollers, they should be used with discretion. Most people find the hot brush easier to handle as the bristles grip the hair. Curling tongs require more expertise, and if you're new to tongs practise handling

5

6

barrel of the curling tongs or the heat will not penetrate the hair evenly.

Allow every section to cool before combing, and dress out as normal.

Latest innovations on the market are spiral rods and shapers; an up-date on the old method of setting with rags. This newest form of roller is reminiscent of the old bendy toys and consists of a piece of wire covered with a hard wearing, pliable, rubberised material, around which the hair is wrapped.

For medium to long hair, this new concept in rollers is ideal. Used on dry to damp hair, the results are amazing, transforming poker-straight hair to a mass of curls in minutes. Not only do

7

8

Kay flicked the ends of the shorter hair for a softer, more textured effect.
7. *The ends of the ponytail can be left curly, or twisted together into a neat bun.*
8. *The use of hair ornaments adds an oriental touch. From shaggy to sophisticated in eight easy stages.*

them, going through the curling motions without heat. When you use them try to keep the ends of your hair smooth around the barrel (round part) or you will end up with the frizzies.

For shorter styles begin at the front; longer hair should be sectioned into four and, starting at the nape, worked forwards over the head. Never take large sections thicker than the diameter of the they work well but they also look attractive and colourful in the hair.

To use, section the hair beginning at the nape. Take a small mesh and twist-wind it around the roller, not layer over layer but to form a spiral along the roller. Bend the end of the roller over to secure. Repeat for the whole head. The degree of curl will depend on your hair texture, how damp your hair was to start with and how long you leave them in.

Spiral rods in lightweight plastic produce a similar effect. Resembling a long corkscrew, the hair is wound round following the screw mouldings, and secured with a special clip.

To dress out, use your fingers to split

the ringlets, or an Afro comb for a fuller effect. Brushing will make the hair wider and fluffier. These new rollers are still only available by mail order from leading salons.

Not everyone with wavy of curly hair appreciates the effect. If you prefer a straighter look without the hassles of blow-drying try a Wrap Round. All you need are two large rollers, some clips, and Scotch tape. Shampoo and towel dry your hair, apply setting lotion and comb through. Part off two sections on the crown, and wind each one around a roller. The remaining hair is combed, section by section, smoothly around the head. As you work, use clips to hold the

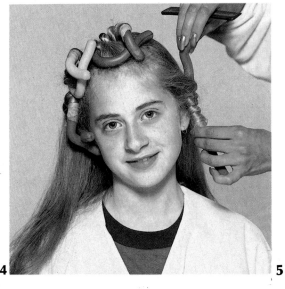

1. *Teenagers love long hair, but they also like a change now and then, and fourteen-year-old Deborah is no exception.*

2. *With clean, dry hair, begin either at the front or in the nape. Section your hair as if for a large roller, twist the section, and wrap the ends in a square of damp tissue.*

3. *Place the ends two-thirds of the way down the shaper and start to wind the hair around, forming a spiral.*
Continue winding down. If the twist begins to unwind turn the shaper until it coils tightly again.

4. *The spiral effect is clearly visible filling the centre of the shaper. Now fold the ends over to secure.*

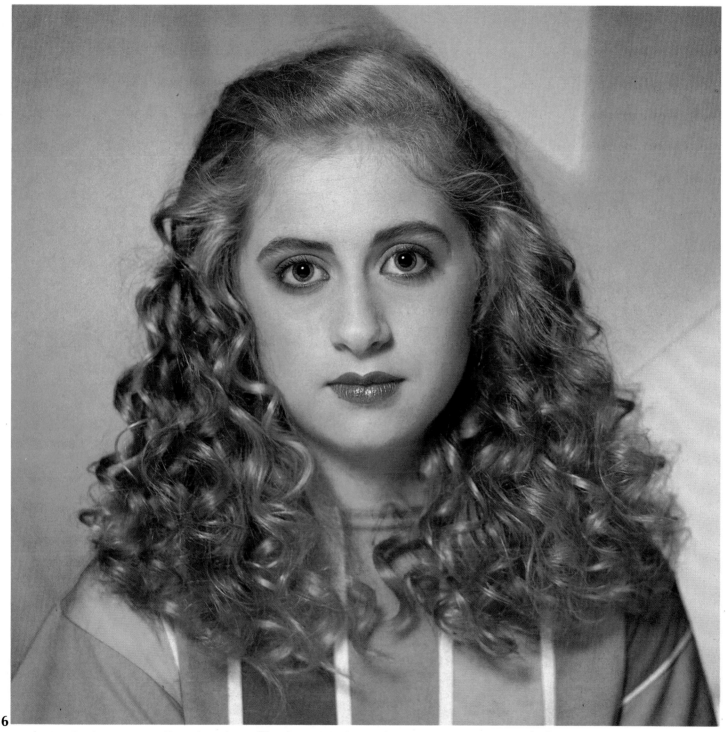

6

5. *The finished set. For a really curly style, the shapers are comfortable enough to sleep in, or if your hair curls easily then thirty minutes under a warm dryer should suffice.*

6. *To dress out – unwind the shapers and pull the ringlets apart with your fingers. A comfortable and easy way to achieve a temporary curly look.*

hair. Once all the hair is wrapped, remove the clips and fasten with Scotch tape. Cover with a hair-net. When your hair is nearly dry reverse the direction of the wrap, so that it falls evenly when dressed out. Finally, brush firmly and you should have a lovely, sleek, glossy style. Your head has just acted as the largest roller you could ever use.

Whichever technique you choose to style your hair, do ensure that everything is kept clean – not only brushes and combs but rollers and pins which get grubby and dusty too. A pretty bag or decorative box keeps your hairstyling kit tidy, dust-free and instantly ready for use.

14
The Answer lies in the Cut

In the early-Sixties a revolution took place; hair became free from backcombing, lacquer and from being forced into an unnatural shape. One man decided that the answer to any successful style lay in the cut. That man was Vidal Sassoon. Hairdressers and public alike responded enthusiastically to his ideas, and British hairdressing has since become synonymous with expert cutting and styling.

Whether you prefer a perm, roller set or blow-dry, the foundation for your style must be a first-class haircut. A good cutter will use your hair in much the same way as a sculptor uses wood or clay, creating a form which is both pleasing to the eye and practical for you. The line of the style should be apparent after the

1. *An unflattering pudding-basin shape, that is far too severe for Maria.*
2. *Line, balance, shape and texture reveal haircutting as an art form.*

cut, prior to drying; the setting/drying method employed only helps to emphasise that line, not create it.

A good cut will last from four to six weeks depending on the shape and length of the hair. The shorter, more defined designs definitely need cutting at least once a month to keep them at their best. Remember that your hair

grows approximately half an inch per month and this extra length can totally alter the balance and line of some styles.

Even if you are growing your hair, or if it is already long, regular cutting is essential. The ends of long hair may be several years old, and during that time will have been exposed to rigorous washing, brushing and drying. Damaged

1. *Permed a month ago, Una's hair looked untidy and rather flat. It is often difficult to decide what to do when your hair is such an in-between length.*

2. *A square layered bob, graduated into the neck, is the perfect answer. Not too short, the shape makes the most of the remaining perm, and skilful use of bleach brightens up a rather drab colour.*

and split ends can be kept at bay with regular trims every six weeks.

Always try to have your hair cut wet. It is much easier to produce an accurate cut on clean, wet hair. Your stylist may allow your hair to dry out as he or she works, particularly if it is curly or wavy. In this way they can see how the shape is progressing and work with the natural lie of your hair. From the hairdresser's point of view it is also far more pleasant and hygienic working on clean hair, as you can imagine.

Razors and electric clippers have gained in popularity recently, and some stunning looks have originated from their use. But in the main, do beware of letting someone loose on your hair with one of these implements. Very few haircuts need thinning all over and what little is required can be done with the points of the scissors, employing a method called pointing or pruning.

5

6

7

8

3. Sarita has pretty but flat hair which over emphasises a square face shape, a fuller style will soften the shape. A razor is to be used to achieve soft layers, but first the hair needs perming to encourage root lift (see permanent waving).

4. Beginning at the sides, the hair is combed forward and cut, paradoxically this encourages the hair to move back away from the face.

5. Gradually the length increases towards the nape area. As you can see, a razor cut need not mean short, chewed-looking hair.

6. Now the front hair is directed forward and blended with the sides.

7. For height the top is cut fairly short, but it must still blend with the sides and back.

8. Finally the perimeter shape is checked and left almost the same length, as requested by Sarita.

9. Shyloks foam massaged through, and then blow-dried using the fingers to pull the hair straight up. The finished result is a shape that lengthens and slims Sarita's face, and a perfect example of an excellent professional razor cut.

9

1. *The result of a good professional cut, with shape established. Dawn's hair was wet cut into place. The wet hair was combed into place and the setting began at the front, following the wet design. When the top and crown were completed her short hair was dried flat. The smoothest rollers were used wherever possible, and the ends of her hair wrapped neatly around each roller. When Dawn's hair was completely dry the rollers were removed and the hair brushed thoroughly, backcombed lightly at the roots, and with her fingers and a comb, the ends were flicked into place.*

Cutting your own or a friend's hair is a definite NO. It takes years of experience to produce a good cutter, so leave it to the experts and keep your friends. A disastrous experiment can take months to grow out, therefore it is worth every penny to include the cost of a professional haircut in your monthly budget.

Sometimes people are confused about trims and haircuts. To a hairdresser the difference between the two is minimal. The same procedure has to be gone through whether you are removing ten inches or half an inch, which is why the word trim is not now so widely used. A cut is a cut regardless of the amount taken off, and consequently the price reflects the work involved.

As we get older the tendency is to avoid certain haircuts, because we feel they are too young, or we stick with the same style for years, which can be even more ageing. The secret is to soften the line and steer clear of straight, geometric shapes. Today's haircuts are very versatile, and it's amazing how a light perm can transform a younger, severe look into a flattering, feminine design suitable for the mature woman, whilst maintaining the modern form.

A new haircut is very personal, so choose your hairdresser with care. Follow some of the advice in the chapters entitled "You and Your Hair" and "Choosing a New Hairstyle". By all means take a picture with you if you feel it will help, but don't expect to come out as a cloned version of the model in the photo. After all, it would be very boring if we all looked like Sue Ellen Ewing or Princess Diana, so why try? Think of your "Total Image" and be an individual.

Blow drying your hair should be easy – ninety per cent of the work is in the cut, and drying adds the finishing touch. Before you start, assemble everything you will need: a comb with large and fine teeth, sectioning clips, brushes and a blow-dryer. An additional word on brushes; choose ones that move easily through the hair without snarling or catching. A Denman or similar type is fine (available from leading chemists and salons). Round brushes of various diameters are useful for more curly styles. Finally, a vent brush, which has wide gaps between uneven quills, helps to create a lovely ripple effect through layered haircuts.

After shampooing and conditioning, rough-dry your hair using a warm dryer to remove excess moisture. Lift the hair with your fingers to allow the air to circulate. Keep the dryer moving all the time to avoid concentrating too much heat in one area.

When the hair is damp comb through and divide into sections – two sides, top, crown and nape.

Begin at the nape, working on the hair section by section. First, blow-dry against the natural growth for more lift at the roots, then bring the hair down in layers, turning the brush in the hair as you do so to produce more curl and bend in the ends.

Work through the back and crown, layer by layer, keeping the dryer moving all the time. Try not to aim the air from ends to roots, but always down the hair shaft. This prevents raising of the cuticle which will make your hair look dull, besides damaging it. Proceed to the side sections, and reverse the dry as before, then gradually bring the hair down, rotating the brush as you work. Now blow-dry the top, mesh by mesh. Brush into shape, and if any more curl is needed in the ends or fringe, work

---

2. *To achieve a full, but soft, shape on medium-length, layered hair requires a little time and effort, but the results are well-worthwhile. Choose a round brush to give curl as well as root lift. Caroline has already completed the left side. The right side will be dried in the same way.*

3. *On the top take sections the same diameter as your brush. Wrap the hair around keeping the ends smooth. Keep rotating the brush in the hair, to speed up drying and prevent heat damage.*

4. *Once the top and crown are dry work down to the fringe. Still take small sections, and keep that dryer moving all the time.*

5. *Proceed to the sides rolling the hair back to flick away from the face.*

6. *Finish drying the sides and continue in this manner to the centre back. If you prefer, complete both sides and back leaving the top until last. For hair that drops quickly it is advisable to clip each section into place as it is dried.*

7. *For more volume lightly backcomb your hair before smoothing into shape. If you have thick or coarse hair, a good brush through with a vent brush, to accentuate the layers will be sufficient.*

2

3

4

5

6

7

1

1. *Looking at Jacqueline's hair it's hard to believe how naturally curly it really is.*
2. *Once the hair is cut shorter on top and around the face the natural curl just bounces back. Layered throughout and left to dry naturally, the style relies purely on the cut to create this lovely shape.*
3. *Fine straight hair requires a more definite shape to keep it neat and tidy all day, a fact that Paula, as a dancer, was aware of only too well.*
4. *A simple, but perfectly executed, strong bob. Totally one length, the hair will always fall back into place no matter how hectic the going gets.*

3

2

4

around the perimeter of your shape using a smaller radial brush for extra bounce. Direct the air onto the brush, but still keep air and brush moving all the time. Don't over-dry your hair. Keep a water spray handy to re-damp any section that has dried out too quickly.

This is the basic method of blow-drying for average length hair; with some styles you may start from the top or front. When you next visit the salon for a cut, watch the stylists at work, you will pick up a lot of helpful tips which can be tried out at home.

Finger and scrunch drying are great techniques for short or longer layered cuts. To finger dry, keep lifting the hair from the roots; the heat from your hands and the atmosphere dries the hair in the most natural way possible, without artificial heat. For more fullness and body use a blow-dryer, and scrunch the hair up in your hand as you move the warm air over your head.

Finally, don't forget to use a blow-dry lotion, a little gel or mousse if your hair is fine and fly-away.

15
Girls who Wear Glasses

Not everybody has given up wearing glasses in favour of contact lenses. In fact, some people who have been wearing glasses for most of their lives look quite strange without them.

We nearly all wear glasses at one time or another, either because we have to or to protect our eyes from the harsh glare of natural and artificial light. Whatever the reason, I am sure you find choosing new frames a confusing and expensive experience.

Your hairstyle is probably the last thing you think of when arranging an appointment with your optician. Obviously the most important thing on your mind is that the correct lenses are prescribed for you. But after all the tests and eye charts comes the moment of decision; the time to choose your frames.

The shape of your face is the first physical aspect you should consider; choose frames that complement your bone structure and fit securely over your nose and ears. If you usually wear make-up then do so when trying on new frames, if only to ensure that colours don't clash.

As with make-up, wear your hair in its normal style for the appointment. Once you have narrowed down your choice of frames to five or six, check that the shape and proportion of the glasses, in relation to your face, are not thrown out of balance by your hairstyle. This will help you to narrow your selection even further. If you like to change your style frequently then play around with your hair – brush it forward, back, to the side, behind the ears. Is the whole picture still aesthetically pleasing no matter which

Remember Sarah? We think you will agree that her specs fulfil all the requirements outlined in this chapter.

way you dress your hair? Eliminate the frames which do not allow for any versatility. Don't feel embarrassed when you have to wear glasses every day; it is important that you make the right decision.

The colour of your frames should take hair colour into account. As a rule choose neutral shades of browns, beiges and greys. Slightly pearlised tones can be very flattering for the more mature woman. Strong colours such as bright red, green and blue can be fun and fashionable. However, weird colours and

eccentric designs tend to date very quickly and unless you are prepared to purchase according to fashion, beware of gimmicky frames.

Lots of glitter and rhinestones can put a little sparkle into your life but avoid overdoing the effect. Stick to just one or two discreetly placed stones which catch the light as you move.

Having made your final selection, try on the frames in front of a full-length mirror. Do the glasses complement and enhance your total look? If so, then you have made the right choice.

When having you hair cut or styled, tell the hairdresser that you wear glasses. Don't hide them away in your handbag, donning them only as you walk out. He or she may ask you to put them on before proceeding to cut or set. Wide flick-ups at ear level could look disastrous with bat-wing specs. If you have your hair roller-set and want to read under the dryer, ask if you can wear your glasses. The stylist may request that you don't, or will assist you to put them on without disturbing the rollers or curls over the ears. Many a set has been ruined by carelessly jammed on glasses.

Finally, try to allow yourself plenty of time when trying on new specs. If you need extra advice, take a friend along who will give you an honest opinion. Do remember to wear make-up and style your hair as normal. If you look a mess then nothing is going to suit you.

Glasses certainly do make some people look more attractive, and the women I know that wear them have definitely disproved the old saying, "Men never make passes at girls who wear glasses".

16
Permanent Waving

1

2

3

Perming techniques and products have changed dramatically since the days when grandma was wired up to the ceiling, plugged in and left to frizz. Now you have the choice of soft curls, a partial perm, or just root lift depending on the final style. With many of today's popular easy care styles permanent waving is a must, but in most cases the curl looks so natural that you could be forgiven for asking, "Does she or doesn't she?".

Whether you need a perm or not will depend on your hair type and style. If you have fine, limp, flat hair, a perm will add body, enhance the cut, and generally alter the texture, making each hair feel a little coarser and thicker. Greasy hair will seem less so, as the perm lifts the hair away from the scalp and slightly dries it.

The length of your hair is very important. Short to medium-length layered looks respond well to perming, giving overall fullness. It is possible to perm long, one-length hair and achieve a good wave pattern from root to tip, but if you desire more lift on the crown, then some layering will be needed through the top, otherwise the weight of your hair will pull it down flat to the scalp.

Hair condition is a key factor in perming. If your hair is dry, brittle and split, regular conditioning treatments and a good cut will be required before a perm is attempted. Any old perm left in the hair is best cut-off before re-perming. Tinted hair is especially fragile, having been subjected to one chemical process already, and needs careful, experienced handling.

Perming is out of the question for the complete bleached blonde, unless you want to end up looking like walking candy floss, or worse. Henna can make perming difficult as the lotion cannot penetrate the hair shaft properly. Try to leave at least two months between a henna application and perming.

Perming your hair is a chemical process which can be potentially dangerous and damaging. So if in doubt, and assuming you can afford it, opt for the professional treatment. Hopefully you will have read the previous chapters about your hair and choosing a hairdresser. Remember to visit the salon several times before booking for a permanent wave.

During these visits, ask your stylist's

advice. He or she may have already suggested a perm. Once the decision has been made you will need to talk to the person who is actually going to do it. In some salons the stylist will also perm your hair, in others a specialist permer takes care of all the perming carried out in that salon. During the consultation your hair and scalp will be examined and a test curl may be taken. You will be asked questions about what home products you have used or are using; advised on home hair care prior to the perm; told the effects that the chemicals will have on it, and what sort of after-care routine you should follow. The salon will either retail a range of conditioning products and shampoos, or will recommend suitable treatments that can be purchased from the chemist. Don't be surprised if you are asked about your general health and whether you have been taking any medication for a long time. It's all relevant. Beware the permer who asks nothing and explains even less, or can't even be bothered to talk to you. Take your custom elsewhere.

Once the consultation is over, the next step is the perm itself. Cutting and perming now go hand in hand. Many styles are cut before and after waving to achieve the best effect. Your stylist will discuss with the permer his interpretation of the finished style, and after the shampoo and preliminary cut, the permer takes over.

A pre-perm conditioner may be applied first to even out the porosity and protect your hair. Next, the hair is sectioned and wound onto perm rods. In some salons perm lotion is applied as shape of the perm rod. Regular tests should be taken to ensure that it does not over-process. When ready, the hair is rinsed for at least five minutes with the curlers still in place. Excess water is gently removed with a towel, and the second

4

1. *During the consultation Caroline discussed the problems she encounters with her heavy, flat, straight hair, and her ideas of a suitable style – soft, full shape, versatile, easy to manage and above all, not too short.*

2. *Before shampooing, the hair is analysed and the correct perm lotion chosen. After a gentle shampoo, the hair is then directionally wound onto large perm rods, and lotion applied to each curler.*

3. *Fifteen minutes later and the hair is ready to be rinsed, with the rods still in place, then blotted with a towel. Next, neutralizer is spread evenly over every curler. After approximately five minutes all the perm rods are removed and additional neutralizer applied for a further five minutes.*

4. *With the hair rinsed and conditioned, we have a lovely soft curl. Before drying, the top layers are to be cut shorter and weight removed from the fringe.*

5. *With a little instruction Caroline blow-dried her own hair (see: 'The Answer Lies In The Cut'); the finished result proves what a difference a good permanent wave can make.*

5

the hair is wound, but many now favour the post damping method, applying lotion when the winding is complete. The perm lotion now goes to work, penetrating through the cuticle into the cortex of the hair. It starts breaking down some of the internal links (sulphur bonds) which hold the hair in its natural form. Your hair now begins to take on the stage, neutralizing, commences. The neutralizer reforms the majority of the bonds into their new pattern. Neutralizer is put onto every perm curler and left for several minutes. The curlers are then removed and more neutralizer applied. Finally, the hair is rinsed, conditioned and you are returned to your stylist for the final cut or set.

If during any of the processes you feel the slightest sensation of burning or irritation, speak up loudly. A burned scalp is too high a price to pay for curly hair.

If you experience any problems with your perm, such as its being too soft or too frizzy, then go back to the salon. Don't be fobbed off with excuses. Any problems should have been discussed and explained during the consultations. In some salons free treatments and styling services will be offered until the condition improves, or it may be possible to re-perm or relax the curl depending on the problem and state of your hair.

Professional permers employ many different techniques when winding a perm. They are a far cry from the straight

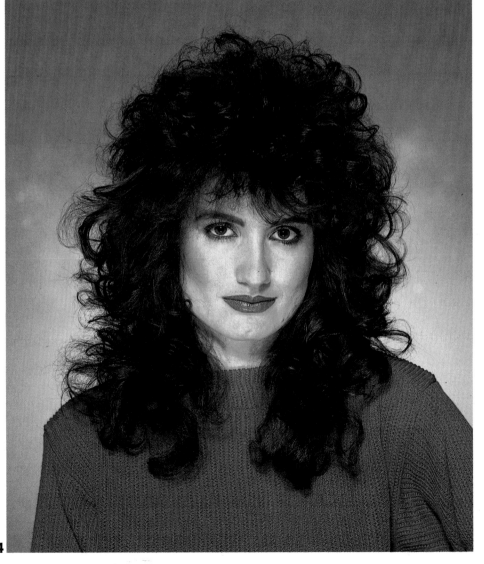

1. *It is not always necessary to perm all of the hair, as we proved with Susie, who felt that she only needed more height and a softer fringe.*

2. *A partial perm on the top adds body and eliminates the parting. This was followed by a warm brown semi-permanent colour to enhance the natural tones.*

3. *Layered throughout, blending to the original length and razor cut at the front for a softer fringe, the style is completed by the application of foam mousse and scrunch drying (notice how the hair is rolled up in the hand).*

4. *A partial perm is not suitable for every head but it is well-worth enquiring; for Susie it was the perfect solution to her problem.*

5

6

back and down method normally associated with perming.

Directional perm winding follows the line of the style, almost as if it were being set, and is great for short styles as it helps the hair to fall easily into place.

Fine hair may be weave permed to create as much fullness as possible. A mesh the same size as the perm curler is parted off. Some of the hair is then woven out using the tail of a comb. The hair below the comb is wound onto a larger curler, leaving out the woven meshes. This is repeated several times until a large section has been completed. The remaining meshes are now wound onto smaller curlers. Sometimes the woven meshes are left totally straight for a more tousled, wild look. In some salons the term "Piggy Back Wind" is used to describe this technique, simply because one curler sits on top of the other, in the same section.

Root perms are very popular. The ends of the hair are left free and straight. The curler is put into the hair up to an inch or two from the ends and wound down to the roots. It can look alarming when you see yourself with tufts of hair sticking out from each curler, but if you want a straighter effect with lots of root lift this is the perfect method.

These are a few of the methods used for winding perms. There are hundreds of permutations. Knowing which method

5. Masses of large curlers wound on tiny sections in this very natural fashion, will provide the strong root lift required for Sarita's new style.
6. Razor cut and then finger dried with the blow-dryer, the degree of lift produced by the perm is easy to see.

to use and when takes a good deal of experience and knowledge, so for fashion technique leave perming to the professionals.

Home perms, are they good or bad? On the whole, modern home perm kits are extremely good. After all, they wouldn't be so popular or sell so well if they were not. The problem lies not so much with the product as the way in which it is used.

The new soft perms have caused a revolution in home perming. Being free from ammonia they don't smell as bad as the early types, and the resulting curl is soft and natural.

Because of the change in formulation the degree of curl produced is far less than with the old perm kits and therefore more suitable for today's styles. One drawback is that the curl does not seem to last very long, although in this respect they are improving all the time.

If you have a fairly simple style and want to try a home perm, enlist the aid of a friend who can put rollers in neatly and help rinse your hair. Have your hair cut by

your hairdresser into a neat, even shape before perming; this will help when winding the curlers. Prepare everything you will need, especially plenty of towels. Now sit down and read the directions several times, keeping them handy for reference. Doing a test curl is always advisable, and you will find instructions for such tests in the leaflet.

Section your hair and wind each section methodically onto the perm curlers. Try to keep the ends smooth over the curler; once they are twisted or buckled there is only one way to remove them – by cutting.

Follow the directions implicitly; they are based on the experience of years of research so don't alter them. One young lady I met recently thought she knew better and left the perm curlers and lotion in overnight. Her long hair resembled a scouring pad, completely matted. My colleague had no choice but to cut her hair very, very short.

Providing you follow each step precisely your home perm should be fine. Do keep your style simple, and don't be too disappointed if it does not look as professional as you had hoped, or like the girl on the packet. Those hairstyles are permed and dressed by professional hairdressers; the model probably doesn't even know one end of a perm curler from the other.

Most of the manufacturers have advisory services for the general public, so if you meet with any problems, contact them. You will find the address on the packet or instruction sheet.

Whether you perm your hair at home or go to a salon, treat it with respect. Wash with a mild shampoo for permed hair, and always use conditioner. If the hair is very dry use a moisturising protein treatment to restore elasticity and reduce dryness. Avoid using curling tongs or heated rollers unless really desperate. Have your hair cut every four to six weeks; extra length soon drags the curl down.

Look after your hair, keep it in tip-top condition, and it's unlikely that new acquaintances will ever suspect that your hair is not naturally curly.

17
Colour Ways

From the ancient Egyptians through to the present day, women have been fascinated at the prospect of being able to change their natural hair colour. None of us it seems, is satisfied with nature's handiwork. Beneath every brunette lurks a vibrant red-head just waiting to be set free.

1. *'A suitable case for treatment' aptly applies to Loraine's hair. Returning multi-coloured bleached hair to a more natural shade presents special problems, and is definitely best left to the professionals.*
2. *The first step involves replacing the red pigment removed during bleaching. This may look dramatic, but it is really necessary if the final colour is to hold and look natural.*
3. *With the hair tinted a good, even red*

shade it is now possible to apply the final colour – in this case a mixture of light brown and red. Towards the end of development the front hair is released and tinted a light copper.
4. *A long and delicate process, be prepared to spend most of the day in the salon if you have a similar problem. Even so the result is well-worth the time and money as our before and after pictures prove.*

Whether you colour your hair at home or go to a salon, there are a few important questions you should ask yourself before beginning.

Is My Hair In Good Condition? If you have dry, brittle, permed or relaxed hair, keep colouring simple. Avoid permanent tints which tend to dry the hair further or go to a professional colourist who has the experience to cope with your problem. Take his advice, and if he recommends that you do not use any colour products for the time being, don't rush to the nearest unscrupulous salon where they will colour your hair regardless of the consequences.

With dry, porous hair the cuticle is

raised along the hair shaft, which allows the colour to penetrate unevenly, resulting in a patchy appearance. The cuticle also needs to be closed to absorb and reflect light, the primary source of all colour. Therefore, if your hair is dull and rough, any colour you use is not going to show to its maximum potential.

How Can I Enhance The Natural Glints In My Hair? Try a colour shampoo. Available in small sachets, they are easy to use, just like a normal shampoo, except that the second lather is left on for five to ten minutes.

Instructions are printed on the back of each sachet, including information on which one to choose to enhance your natural shade. Do not use them on

previously tinted or bleached hair unless it is in very good condition, or recommended on the pack. At the salon your stylist may suggest a temporary colour; this is also known as a water rinse. Very mild, they coat the outside of the hair shaft and are easily removed by shampooing. They are perfect for masking yellow tones in white hair, toning brassy blonde, or blending-in the odd grey strand.

How Can I Cover My Grey Hair? Simple – a semi-permanent colour is the answer. This type penetrates further into the hair than temporary colour and, as a rule, lasts from six to eight shampoos. Choose a colour as near as possible to your natural shade, (nothing red or gold).

Don't go too dark or it will look harsh against your skin tone. Most semi-colours are applied to clean, damp hair and massaged through like a shampoo. After developing, add a little water and lather up the colour; rinse until the water runs clear.

Read the instruction leaflet carefully, and always carry out a skin test.

I Would Like To Have A Colour, But Nothing Permanent. Try a semi-permanent as for grey hair. You will find some lovely chestnut and mahogany shades available to brighten up drab hair. This type of colour is perfect for the person who is nervous of trying a permanent colour. Use as above according to the enclosed instructions.

1

mix several shades together extends the range still further. All good reasons for choosing a professional service as opposed to home colouring.

If you want to use a permanent colour at home, don't go for a drastic change; one or two shades lighter or darker is sufficient. The more you change your natural colour, the more complicated it gets. The easiest home permanent tints to use are the shampoo-in ones but if you can enlist the aid of a friend to apply the colour section by section, you will be far happier with the result.

Regrowth needs attention every four to six weeks, and is often more complicated to do than the first

2

3

4

Certain shampoo-in colours give the impression that they are semi-permanents, but beware if they claim to lighten or alter your natural shade; this is permanent colour. Read the back carefully and always carry out a skin test.

Can I Completely Change My Hair Colour? Complete changes usually involve permanent tints, which penetrate the cortex and actually alter the natural colour molecules in the hair shaft. Permanent tints can be difficult to apply, and choosing the right colour can be a very hit and miss affair.

In the salon, a tint is applied to dry, unwashed hair which has been carefully

1. Welcome to the wonderful world of colour.
2. A few highlights remain in Corine's hair but they are hardly noticeable. As a singer she needs a far more dramatic colour to show under strong stage lights.
3. Staying with highlights we used the weaving technique and tinfoil, which is still one of the best and most accurate methods of highlighting.

sectioned. It is put on evenly and methodically with a small brush. Also, the range of colours available to the professional is far greater than to the consumer, and the colourist's ability to

4. Back completed – two shades of tint have been used alternately to highlight the back hair. While on the top some of the meshes will be bleached to produce a stronger shade variation.
5. Here you can see how precisely the technician needs to work. Hair is woven out from a fine section.
6. The woven hair is then laid onto a strip of tinfoil and tint or bleach applied; finally

application. Care must be taken to apply colour to the new growth only. Many consumer tints state that there is no need to worry about retouching; simply apply all over as before. Fine in theory, but not in

5

6

7

the foil is folded into a neat parcel and the hair left to develop.

7. *Foil removed, shampooed, conditioned and blow-dried. A lengthy and meticulous process, but when the subtle shades of blonde mingling with the natural hair colour produce such a dramatic change, it is money and time well-spent.*

practice. You can end up with a very patchy result – the ends getting darker or lighter as the colour builds up.

As before, follow the instructions and carry out a skin test.

What About Bleaching? Not many people completely bleach their hair these days and if you are contemplating such a drastic step, go to a professional colourist. Bleaching is reserved mainly for highlights and special effects. A more natural blonde result can be achieved with certain high lift tints providing your hair is no darker than dark blonde.

The darker your natural shade, the less likely it is that bleached hair will suit you. To bleach dark, resistant hair very powerful chemicals are needed, and for obvious reasons these are only available to the professional hairdresser. So it is doubtful that you would achieve a pretty

blonde colour at home anyway.

If you do try home bleaching, definitely carry out a strand test, follow the instructions, and don't forget the skin test.

Could I Try Henna? Henna is a natural vegetable colour made from the leaf of a shrub called *Lawsonia Inermis*. It adds warm red tones to brunette hair (do not use on grey, blonde or bleached hair). Revived in the Sixties because of the interest in natural products, and the sheen it imparted to the hair, it does have its drawbacks. Henna is messy to apply, unpredictable, and although the initial result is good, will often fade, leaving an

1. *"Mousey brown", is Tracey's description of her hair. A semi-permanent colour will soon add depth and interest without permanently altering her natural shade.*
2. *A warm brown colour livens up*

mousey hair and puts back the shine. This particular brand is in a handy dispenser that expels the colour in foam form, making it quick and easy to apply. The whole process will only take about thirty

minutes.
3. *Reshaped and blow-dried the subtle warm tones enhance the natural lights, and the colour can be repeated as often as desired.*

orangey-red hue in the hair.

Never use henna yourself if you have permed or colour treated hair. Seek professional advice. Avoid compound henna like the plague. It contains metallic salts which can react strongly with other hair preparations. Use only pure vegetable henna.

How Do I Give Myself A Skin Test?
1. Clean a small patch behind the ear with surgical spirit.
2. Mix a small amount of the colour to be used.
3. Apply colour behind the ear.
4. Leave for forty-eight hours.
5. Check for any inflammation or irritation. If clear, then it is safe to proceed. Any adverse reaction indicates that you must use no permanent colour whatsoever.

What Colour Will Suit My Complexion? Before choosing, look at your skin under natural light. Are you fair, dark, ruddy or olive skinned?

Reds, chestnuts and golds add warmth to pale skins but avoid them if you have a pink or ruddy complexion:

stick to slightly ashen tones.

Soft, warm browns and burgundy shades complement darker skins. A very light colour is too great a contrast between skin and hair so only lighten one or two shades.

Olive Skins look best with darker shades but do not use anything too red or you may find your complexion takes on a greenish hue.

Pale Complexions can be very dramatic with contrasting dark hair providing strong make-up is worn. Ash blondes make you look even paler, so aim for darker blondes with a hint of gold.

Mature Skin With Grey Hair? Be careful of the colour you select. As your hair gets whiter so your complexion changes, and although you may once have been dark brown, this will no longer suit you. Go instead for a light shade, which will look much softer.

Maintenance. Temporary rinses and colour shampoos are relatively inexpensive and can be used as often as required.

Semi-permanents will last from six to eight shampoos. Salon prices vary, so check that you can afford it first. As there is no regrowth, the need to colour frequently is eliminated which keeps costs down.

With permanent tints again the cost varies. Salons will normally charge more for the first full application, slightly less for regrowths. It is important that retouching is carried out every four to six weeks, so check that you can afford the upkeep first, whether it is a home or salon colour.

Bleaching can be very expensive, and may need retouching every three to four weeks, which is not only damaging for your hair but also your purse, so think twice about this one.

Salon Specials.

Highlights. A popular way of going blonde without regrowth problems. Very fine strands of hair are lightened either to blend or contrast with your natural colour. The fine meshes may be woven out, bleach applied and then wrapped in tinfoil, or a cap with self-

4. *Regrowths always present a problem, none more so than when you want to grow out a previous colour or bleach as does Lisa.*

5. *Highlighting is the solution. Again the weaving technique is employed, but this time only the new growth is coloured. Cling film has uses other than wrapping food and, as it seals itself, is perfect for such delicate work.*

6. *The previously bleached hair remains untouched as the cling film prevents any colour from seeping onto the lengths.*

7. *The entire new growth has been highlighted. In this case it is important not to lighten the hair too much or we defeat the purpose of the exercise.*

8. *The heavy demarcation line disappears as the fine blonde meshes blend in the regrowth. A process that can be repeated until all the bleached hair has been cut out.*

9. *If you like to wear your hair up then make sure that the nape hair is also treated or it will look very dark when exposed.*

4   5   6   7

8   9

sealing holes is put over the hair, and a few strands pulled through each hole with a crochet hook. The visible hair is then tinted or bleached. After bleaching, a toner may be applied to subdue any brassy, yellow tones.

Lowlights. A similar technique to highlights but instead of bleach, warm or darker shades of colour are used to brighten and add more interest to your hair.

Naturalising. A very popular method of adding colour. As before fine meshes of hair are coloured but this time three or four different shades are used. This really increases the glints in your hair, imitating the natural pigmentation which varies all over the head. No head of hair is one total, solid colour.

Highlights, lowlights and naturalising are fairly expensive initially. The advantage is that the regrowth is far less evident and, therefore, only needs doing every three to four months.

Spot Or Finger Colours. A quick and relatively cheap method of hair colouring. The hair is brushed into shape and colour applied with the fingers or brush, to emphasise certain aspects of the style. It can be very subtle or dramatic depending on the style and colours used.

Fantasy Colours. Blue, red, green, pink, or violet. If you feel daring enough anything is possible. These colours are fairly new and became popular with the punk rockers, but used well they can look very attractive. The hair is first bleached to prepare a light base, and then the colour applied. They do tend to fade so will need regular maintenance, although the bleach will not need to be re-done each time.

Whatever type of colour you choose, condition your hair regularly and use a shampoo for colour-treated hair. Strong shampoos soon strip the colour and cause rapid fading.

As you can see, hair colouring is a magical world. It can do wonders for your morale and for your appearance.

1. Debra's hair not only needed cutting, but some form of colour to add interest and accentuate the layers.
2. Rather than tint the whole head, a warm copper colour is applied to the tips of the hair only, which will create a sun-lightened effect. Once all the ends have been tinted and wrapped in foil, the colour is left to develop. You may feel like a christmas-tree but the foil and cotton-wool are to protect the virgin hair.
3. Cut and coloured – the coppery tips ripple through the hair. A great way to experiment with colour as it can soon be cut if you get bored.

18
Keeping it Long

To many people, especially men, long hair conjures up an image of alluring femininity. Indeed, long hair can look very feminine and attractive, but only if it is healthy, perfectly cut and well-cared for. Above all, long hair must suit you.

All of us, usually in our teens, go through a phase of growing our hair, refusing to have it cut, letting it get longer and longer regardless of the split, chewed ends; unwilling to part with one tenth on an inch. All this so that we can say "I've got long hair". Hopefully, we soon pass through this stage, realising that length, in itself, means nothing if it doesn't suit you, if your hair is dry, brittle

4. Long, long hair such as Val's demands a gentle touch to keep it in tip-top condition. A treatment will restore shine and counteract dryness and a trim removes split ends.

5. One hour later and the hair looks and feels like silk. Follow the advice in this chapter and you could possibly have hair like this.

4

5

1. A pretty plait that incorporates just the hairline hair and is suitable for any age group.

and full of split ends or if it is not of the right texture and density for such a style.

Whether you are growing your hair or have always worn it long, get the ends trimmed every six weeks. Split ends do not disappear, the hair just continues to split up the hair shaft.

Washing and drying your hair can be a chore, especially when it blocks the sink as you're trying to rinse. For this reason, shampoo over the bath; your hair will then hang clear of any dirty water. You will definitely need a shower attachment for rinsing.

The tips of your hair may be up to six years old, so remember that pure silk dress I mentioned in the chapter on conditioners, and treat them carefully. Condition after every shampoo, paying particular attention to those fragile ends. A special protein treatment every three

to four weeks helps to strengthen the hair and prevent breakage.

After shampooing and conditioning, pat out as much excess water as you can. Using a wide toothed comb (never a brush) comb through your hair, working from the ends towards the roots. If circumstances permit, allow your hair to dry naturally, finishing off with the blow-dryer to curve the ends up or under.

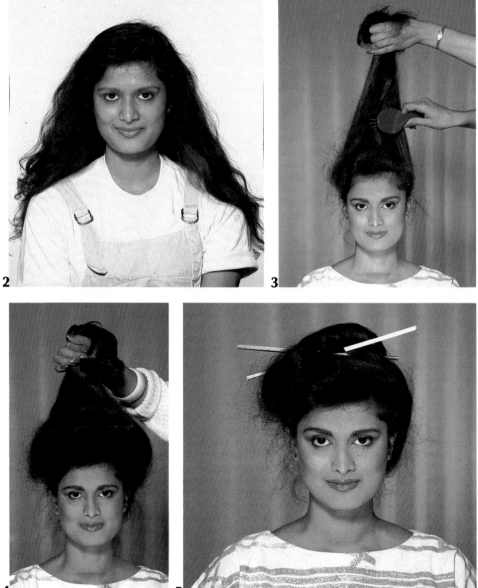

2. Angela has very long dense hair and like many people she hates backcombing, but she would love to wear her hair up in a soft feminine style.

3. Begin by brushing all the hair up into a ponytail, which is not tied but held firmly in the hand.

4. Gently lower the hand towards the crown. The shape fills out as you do so.

5. Twist the ends forward and roll them

under to form an elongated bun shape. Two pins hold the hair in place, one in either end of the roll. Chopsticks are not solely for eating with. Two woven through the roll diagonally help secure the hair and act as a novel form of ornamentation.

6. A selection of combs, slides and pins guaranteed to transform the simplest hairstyle.

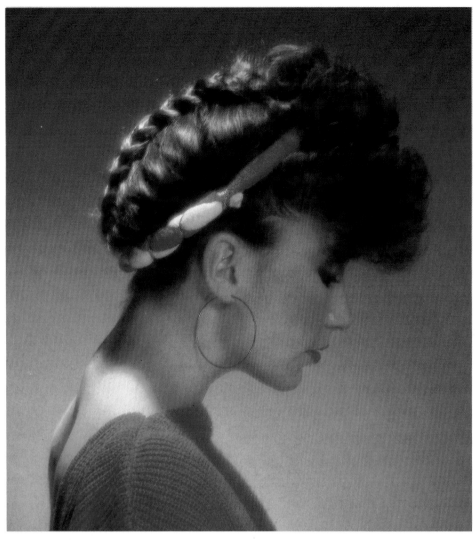

1

1. *Style change for Kay. A reverse plait creates a lot of interest at the back, while the layered front is backcombed into a full quiff. The co-ordinated headband looks pretty but also holds the hair firmly in place.*

2. *Most of us would love very heavy, thick, long hair, but when it comes to an upswept style problems abound, as Tonia has frequently found out.*

4. *Long hair waves so prettily when set on shapers. Paula's hair has been swept back to the crown and pinned, leaving the remaining hair tumbling over her shoulders.*

5. *Two asymmetric ponytails form the base of this design. Spiky swatches of artificial hair pinned into each end of the roll add a touch of individuality for a dramatic look.*

6. *Take care if you blow-dry your long locks, direct heat is notoriously damaging.*

3

Drying heat is one of your hair's main enemies, so keep the use of electrical appliances to a minimum.

If your hair is really long, never attempt to perm or colour it at home. Even a professional may advise against any form of chemical processing, and if they are unwilling to take the risk, and refuse your money at the same time, you should listen to their advice.

Dressing your own hair into an upswept style is not as difficult as you may think. A simple ponytail can become an elegant *chignon* with just a twist of the wrist and a couple of hair ornaments. For ponytails, always use a covered elastic band, and remove them with care. On your next shopping trip visit the big stores and salons, and treat yourself to some of the lovely slides and combs now available. They are so handy

2

3. *Innovative rollers (shapers), the perfect answer to curling long hair.*

for hiding unsightly grips and pins.

A padded roll is a useful accessory for fine hair as it adds fullness without excessive backcombing. If you can't find one to purchase, then make your own by filling part of a stocking with loosely packed cotton-wool until it resembles a fat sausage. This can now be pinned into your head where the roll or twist is to be, and the hair dressed over the padding.

4

5

6

Lovely, long, curly hair is currently very popular, and thanks to some clever hairdressers, easy for you to do at home. In the chapter on setting I told you about a new type of roller, around which you wind a twisted section of hair. They can be used on slightly damp hair for plenty of movement, or on dry hair for a quick boost, and are much quicker than trying to set long wet hair, and sitting for hours under a dryer wearing uncomfortable rollers. If you can't find these rollers to buy, take a leaf out of grandma's book and use rags. To dress out, pull the curls apart with your fingers, starting from underneath and working up over the head. A brush will create a fuller, more fluffy style. To avoid tangles pull apart each section as you remove it from the rollers or rags.

Once the curls are in place, add a touch of extra glamour by twisting some wide ribbon or silk scarves around your head, like a rope, or lightly spray with glitter, and you're ready for a night on the town.

19
Black is Beautiful

Not so long ago the range and availability of products suitable for black hair was very limited. Now, thanks mainly to our American cousins, that situation is rapidly changing. In the Fifties and Sixties very few salons catered specifically for

hair loss. To remove them a strong detergent shampoo was needed and consequently you soon ended up back at square one, with dry hair and an itchy scalp. Fortunately, modern preparations are far lighter and readily absorbed by

programme, which must be adhered to after any chemical process such as relaxing or perming. Always follow their directions, as any deviation may affect the permanency of the process.

6. If you have a very dry scalp, try one of

black hair. This meant that those people who had recently taken up residence in the U.K. had two choices, to do their hair at home or wear a wig, neither option being very satisfactory. As a new generation emerged, born and bred in the U.K., the demand for more professional hair products and services grew. Salons opened to cater to this demand and at last, chemists and department stores included black hair care products on their shelves.

Condition. A dry scalp – fragile and dry hair are just a few of the problems you have to contend with, which is why regular conditioning is of paramount importance. As with any type of hair, a healthy and balanced diet is essential. But black hair has special needs, because it rapidly looses moisture and is very susceptible to atmospheric conditions.

Thick oils and greases used to be applied to combat dryness and protect the hair. Unfortunately, they also clogged the hair follicles, which often resulted in

the hair, making them easier and more pleasant to use.

Basic Maintenance Procedure.
1. Always shampoo with a mild shampoo that will not strip the hair of its natural oils (not baby shampoo).
2. Condition after every shampoo. If your hair is very dry or chemically damaged, use a restructuring protein treatment every two weeks, alternating with a hot oil treatment, which is extremely beneficial.
3. Moisturise every day. These light oils come in handy aerosol cans. Try not to be too heavy-handed when you spray – just a light film over the hair is sufficient.
4. To protect your hair use a reversion resistant hair spray. This will help to prevent your hair from absorbing moisture in the atmosphere and reverting back to its pre-styled state. It also seals the hair against loss of precious natural moisture.
5. Some manufacturers and hairdressers recommend a definite set conditioning

1. Black hair requires firm but delicate handling. Dawn keeps her long hair under control by plaiting it into a tight chignon. Wary of any chemical process, she prefers the temporary method of relaxing, achieved with curling tongs.
2. The clean dry hair is divided into easy to control sections.
3. It is very important to protect and moisturise the hair before any operation that involves direct heat so, beginning at the nape, concentrated hair and scalp conditioner is applied.
4. Gradually the whole head is treated in this manner. Not only is the hair protected but scalp irritation soothed.
5. First the tongs are used to smooth and straighten the hair.
6. This means it can be recurled into its new shape, with the tongs or heated rollers. Smoothed then curled, we see the finished set.
7. Front hair is dressed into a sleek, asymmetric line which contrasts nicely with the remaining loosely curled hair. A sleek and soft curl combination.

5

6

7

the special hair and scalp conditioners; they help to reduce excessive irritation and dryness.

Your hairdresser will probably retail a range of products similar to the ones I have described, plus many more for special problems.

Cutting – a perfect hair cut is the second step to a successful style (condition being the first). Whether your hair is natural, relaxed or permed, a good shape is essential. Keep split ends under control with regular trims.

Hot Combing is a method of temporarily relaxing the hair. If you prefer this method, then do invest in an electric hot comb which is thermostatically controlled and safer to use.

Shampoo, condition and dry your hair. Apply a light oil dressing or pressing cream. Divide the hair into five main sections – top, two sides, crown and nape. Work through each section, taking small partings until all the hair is straight. Finally, curl into style using heated rollers or curling tongs.

Relaxing (Straightening) – a chemical and more permanent method of softening the curl. Any chemical process is best left to the professional hairdresser, but this is especially advisable when relaxing delicate Afro hair. Relaxing creams work very quickly, so if you want to try doing your hair at home, then get a friend to help, and follow the directions to the letter.

There are lots of relaxers available and they come in three main strengths:

mild– for fine, damaged or tinted hair.
regular– for normal hair.
super– for coarse, strong hair.

Choose the one most suitable for your hair type. Never relax your hair yourself if it is tinted, permed or in any way damaged. Your scalp must also be in good condition and free from any abrasions or sores.

Before relaxing, apply a little oil or barrier cream around your hairline to protect the skin.

Part your hair into four and apply the relaxer as directed, evenly and

1

2

3

4

5

6

methodically; try not to pull or stretch the hair as you work. Don't over-process or you could find your hair in your hands rather than on your head.

Remember to remove the cream thoroughly before neutralizing, trying to keep the hair as smooth as possible as you rinse. After neutralizing and the final rinse, condition and set.

It is not advisable to blow-dry directly after relaxing, as this puts too much strain on the hair, unless very carefully done by your stylist.

Curly Perms. An exciting innovation has been the introduction of perming products designed for black hair. The method used is similar to that used on Caucasian hair (see permanent waving).

1. *Fine, long and mostly frizzy hair – Andrea is a perfect candidate for a permanent wave to redirect and define the curl.*

2. *After shampooing, a pre-softening gel is applied evenly to all of the hair. Ten minutes later and after a little additional smoothing, it's time to carefully rinse out the gel.*

3. *Now the hair is easier to control, and can be wound onto perm rods following a directional pattern.*

4. *Winding complete – curling lotion is then applied to every single curler and left to process.*

5. *Processing complete we are ready to rinse thoroughly and neutralize. Don't forget to tell your hairdresser if you feel any soreness or stinging during any of*

these processes.

6. *Sprayed lightly with comb-out conditioner and oil sheen, plus a little curl activator to coat and soften the curls, and we are ready for styling.*

7. *Andrea prefers to let her hair dry naturally into masses of tiny, but not oily, ringlets. Small ponytails bound with ribbon control the longer front hair, and a final spray with reversion resistant hairspray completes our sunshine girl.*

8. *An easy style conversion you can try at home. Carefully comb all but the hairline hair up and pin on top of the head. Only comb when and where necessary or your hair will go frizzy. Mould and pin the top hair into shape and redefine the ringlets around the face and nape.*

7

8

would like a temporary change why not try one of the spray-on colours or glitter sprays. They look superb on dark, curly hair.

To keep your hair in perfect shape, here are ten golden rules for home hair care:

1. Condition after every shampoo.
2. Moisturise daily.
3. If you decide to relax your hair at home, enlist a friend's help.

The main difference is that the hair is first pre-softened to remove some of the natural curl and make it more pliable. After rinsing to remove the pre-softening gel, the hair is sectioned and wound onto perm curlers then processed and neutralized according to the manufacturer's instructions. In this way the curl is redirected, becoming softer and more manageable. It is really like reverse perming.

After conditioning the hair can be dried naturally, for a curly effect; roller set; or, providing the condition is satisfactory, blow-dried.

The whole process is so simple and allows you the choice of curly hair one day and a sleeker style the next.

Manufacturers and salons usually supply a small booklet for the client, with advice on the best way to maintain your curly locks. Regular hot oil treatments after shampooing, plus daily applications of moisturising oil spray and curl activator, are the standard recommendations.

Colouring can really bring your hair back to life. Rich reds and burgundy shades look stunning in black hair. If your hair is permed or relaxed, stick to semi-permanent colours or lowlights. Avoid all over permanent tints as they can dry your hair and scalp even more. Bleached tips and highlights should be carried out only by an expert colourist.

Hair in its natural curly state is very difficult to colour at home, so if you

4. Follow manufacturers' directions implicitly. If in any doubt, avoid the treatment.
5. Ask your hairdresser's advice at all times.
6. Alway have a good professional haircut every six weeks.
7. Never bleach your own hair.
8. Keep your hair and scalp plus styling equipment clean.
9. Avoid too much direct heat from curling tongs, hot combs and blow-dryers.
10. Once your hair has been chemically processed in any way, treat it with respect.

20
Dazzling Display

When you're feeling in a flamboyant mood, or your hairstyle is in need of a little added zest, what could be easier than reaching for a can of glitter or coloured spray? Without too much effort you can transform your everyday style into an eye-catching creation, guaranteed to turn a few heads.

You are probably quite familiar with glitter sprays. After all, it is hard to turn on the T.V. or go out dancing without seeing someone twinkling away under the lights. You can achieve that sparkly look in two ways – by using glitter spray or with glitter gel.

The aerosol cans are perhaps the easiest to use. Simply style your hair as normal and spray with glitter, all over or only on the top or sides, One word of advice: wear an old dressing-gown or some sort of covering to protect your outfit when spraying, unless you want to shimmer all over.

Glitter gels are just like the setting gels, but with small particles of glitter suspended in them. As with sprays, the glitter can be white, silver, gold, red or violet, or a combination of all the colours which produces a rainbow effect. The advantage of gel is that you can put the sparkle exactly where you want it – onto the ends of your hair with the fingers; or if you are feeling artistic and have a fairly sleek hairdo, use a fine brush to paint thin lines or swirls of glitter through your hair.

Sprays and gels are also available in fantasy colours; some are even fluorescent – great for being seen in the dark. Spray-on colour can look very attractive if used with discretion. Turning your hair totally fluorescent green may look good for Hallowe'en but not very pretty. Instead, try to spray just the tips of your hair, or put on one or two streaks; a

2 **3**

1. *Make it bold – vibrant coloured spray used only on the front hair, makes for a dramatic style.*

2. *Be daring – add a touch of zest to your style with coloured gel. Simply apply to the hair you want to accentuate with your fingers. And very quickly you'll see the difference. Use just one colour, or several for a rainbow effect.*

3. *Paint it on – sleek styles come alive when coloured gel is applied with a fine brush. Co-ordinate your colours like Dawn and it will look even more striking.*

---

simple idea is to use a stencil. Draw an outline of, say, a butterfly or a flower onto a large sheet of paper. Cut out the shape. Position the stencil over your hair and spray. Remove the paper and, hey presto, you have added your own personal motif to your style.

Coloured gels also come in two forms – normal fashion shades, which may be used all over to enhance the

natural colour (they can be applied before or after styling, as with clear gel), or the more bizarre fluorescent and metallic shades, which are best kept to the tips of the hair. As with the glitter type, coloured gels can be applied with a thin paint brush to create very individual designs.

Generally, the lighter your hair, the more pronounced the effect of the coloured sprays and gels. Be careful if your hair is very dry, porous or bleached, because although they are meant to shampoo out, I have known some cases where several shampoos have been required to remove such colours.

Most of these products are relatively inexpensive (a little goes a long way), and are available from your hairdresser, major chemists and department stores.

You will be amazed at the effects you can create for yourself with just a little practice. By combining glitter and colour, gels and sprays, a hairstyle can become a walking work of art.

21
Holiday Haircare

Lazing on the beach, soaking up the sun, or frolicking in the surf, it's all part and parcel of being on holiday. We know the sun is bad for our skin but very few of us worry about it. Instead, we smother ourselves in oil, lotions and after-sun creams in a vain attempt to cultivate a tan. But what about your hair? It certainly does not benefit from a holiday in the sun, and should be kept covered whenever possible, rinsed thoroughly after swimming and plenty of conditioner applied after every shampoo.

Covering your hair every time you step out into the sun can be a nuisance, and trying to shower after a swim is impossible if you're spending the day on a remote beach. So what can you do to maintain healthy hair? One answer is to opt for a wet-look style. Look around the salons and chemists before you go away, and you will find special gels and conditioners which help to protect your hair from the ravages of sun and sea. Apply liberally, comb into a neat head-hugging shape and then you're ready to face the sun. While you turn a golden brown your hair is being well-conditioned. Remember to rinse it out every evening when you return from the beach. If the wet-look does not appeal to you, then wear a pretty sun hat, or twist a couple of light scarves together and wrap them around your head 'turban style'.

Short hair is definitely easier to handle, and less prone to damage, than long hair. Have your hair cut the week before you leave, preferably into a style which can be naturally dried.

For special nights out, curling tongs and heated rollers can be used to create a sleeker, more dressy style. Remember to check the voltage of all electrical equipment if you're going abroad.

Long hair can also be given the wet-look treatment by day, and transformed into a simple *chignon* or plait for evenings, dressed up with the addition of a pretty comb or flower.

Everyone likes to look their best on holiday, and the tendency is to have a

1. *After swimming rinse and rinse again to remove all traces of chlorine or sea water from your hair.*
2. *Use plenty of conditioner and a sun screen for hair, to protect it from the sun's harsh glare.*

3. *No time to dry your hair? Then gel it and comb into a sleek shape which can be left to dry naturally.*
4. *Evening glamour without hair. Tie a large triangular scarf peasant style, tucking all your hair inside. Twist a long tassled scarf to form a rope and wind it twice round, tying at the side. Co-ordinated with your sun clothes it is also a great way to cover your hair during the day.*

perm or tint right at the last minute. But if you do, beware; your hair is now in a very vulnerable state. Sun and salt water can wreak havoc on chemically processed hair. So if your holiday is to be spent swimming and sunbathing, have a perm several weeks before you depart. This will give your hair a chance to recover. The same applies to tints, although it is often better to leave colouring until you

return, when your colourist can rectify and even out the bleaching effect of the sun.

Don't forget that if your holiday is of the sight-seeing tour variety, strong sunlight can still catch you out, even while you're admiring an ancient monument. Your hair still requires as much attention as if you were on the beach.

Never be tempted to have your hair cut, permed or tinted on holiday. Apart from the language barrier, the stylist does not know you or your hair. Stick to a shampoo and set or blow dry. You will probably find it was just the holiday atmosphere that made you fancy a drastic change of style. That holiday feeling soon disappears, but you can be left with an expensive mistake that may take weeks to grow out.

Finally, take plenty of hair ornaments and pretty silk scarves with you for evening wear; they can add a touch of glamour even to a plain hairstyle. Ribbons and scarves can be plaited into longer hair, or used as a *bandeau*; ornamental combs and slides help keep shorter, unruly hair in place. Glitter sprays and gels liven up simple styles.

Whether it's the South Sea Islands or Torquay, remember to C.P.S.C. every day – Condition, Protect, Shampoo, Condition.

1

2

3

1. *A wet-look style that will stay put through the night's dancing, or comb out plaited hair when dry for an attractive pre-Raphaelite creation.*
2. *Plaits look tidy, yet casual for the beach.*
3. *But if your hair is very long remember to pin up those flowing tresses before tanning or you will end up with a white back.*

22
Those Special Occasions

Perhaps one of the most important days in a person's life is their wedding day. Your appearance is especially important on this unique occasion, and yet things so often go wrong. Head-dresses refuse to stay put; curls drop; bridesmaids hate their hair and in-laws complain that your hairdresser didn't have any idea what an "Italian Style" was. All of these problems are easy to avoid with just a little careful pre-planning.

Head-dresses for the bride and bridesmaids should be purchased well in advance. If garlands of fresh flowers are to be worn in the hair on the day, buy some imitation ones to act as a substitute while you experiment with hairstyles.

Book appointments at the hairdressers for both you and the bridesmaids, not only for the big day, but for several consecutive weeks before. When you go to the salon, explain to the stylist that you are getting married in a few weeks time and would like to try out some different hairstyles, to see which one is going to be most suitable. The stylist will ask to see the head-dresses that you and your bridesmaids propose to wear. This enables him to create styles which will complement your hair and the head-dresses; if you can, describe the dresses as well, particularly the neck line.

During the weeks leading up to the wedding your style will be perfected, or you may prefer to experiment with different styles, leaving the final choice to your hairdresser. By now you should also have a good idea of how long it takes everybody to get their hair done. Don't forget to include the time it takes to drive to and from the salon when working out your final countdown.

Last minute changes, perms or colours, are OUT. Any perming should be carried out at least three weeks prior to the wedding (colours one week).

4

When the bride and bridesmaids visit the salon, seventy per cent of your problems disappear. Well at least you know where everyone is, apart from the groom, of course.

Remember to take your veil along at least once, so that your hairdresser can show you the best way to attach it. Try pinning it on yourself at home as well, walking around to check that it stays put, and to get used to the additional weight and length.

4. *Permed, cut and tinted well in advance, Pam's hair only required blow-drying on the day. A simple classic style that will stay neat and tidy throughout the festivities.*

Tiny tots look delightful as bridesmaids. However, their hair can present a problem. The best advice is to steer clear of fussy styles. Don't drag them into the salon for a scaled-down version of mummy's style. Not only do they get bored and irritable, but nothing looks more ridiculous than a grown up style on a four-year-old's head. Short hair should be clean and neat; longer hair can be worn loose, or in a simple braid or bun if it's fine and straggly. A ring of fresh flowers is all that's needed to complete the picture. Princess Diana's little bridesmaids stole our hearts during the Royal Wedding, and nothing could have been simpler than their natural hairstyles.

1. *It's such an exciting day for two-and-a-half-year-old Isobel, but her simple bob cut will stand up to all that running around. No fussy styles for her, just a tiny half-circlet of flowers pinned on at the last minute and Isobel is ready to capture everybody with her enchanting smile.*

2. *A perfect example of how looking your best can add immeasurably to the excitement and enjoyment of a special occasion.*

3. *Let us not forget the bridegroom. Smart as ever, Philip cuts a dash with his short layered haircut. The only type of style that really looks good with a morning suit.*

4. *Fairy-tale bride, just how everone should look on their wedding day. Linda's heavy top hair has been dressed up, and the remaining hair left to cascade in waves over her shoulders.*

If you are a guest at a wedding or garden party, the chances are that you will be wearing a new hat. As with the bride and bridesmaids, you may need the help of your hairdresser, who will suggest a suitable style and show you how to secure your hat without ruining your hair.

Whatever the special occasion, enlist your stylist's aid; listen to his advice, explain your likes and dislikes. Always take along any hair ornaments you intend to wear. If you are going to style your own hair, choose a design that is neat and easy for you to do; try to experiment a few times before the event. Some of the ideas and techniques shown in previous chapters will help.

Any special day, but particularly your wedding day, should be happy and relaxed with a bride who is beautiful from top to toe. We have told you how to make the most of your hair, the rest is up to you.